THE ULTIMATE BOOK OF

Royal Icing

THE ULTIMATE BOOK OF

Royal Icing

LINDSAY JOHN BRADSHAW

MEREHURST

LONDON

This book is dedicated to Icing Sugar and Egg Whites for the sheer pleasure and enjoyment, knowledge, experience and friends they have given me. LJB.

A standard spoon measurement is used in all recipes.
1 teaspoon = one 5ml spoon
1 tablespoon = one 15ml spoon
All spoon measures are level.

Quantities are given in metric, Imperial and cups.
Follow one set of measures only as they are not interchangeable.

American terms have been included as necessary throughout, given in brackets following the UK name. The following are typical equivalent terms:
cocktail stick – toothpick
icing sugar – confectioner's sugar
greaseproof paper – waxed paper
piping tubes – tips

The author and publisher would like to thank the following:

The Icing Shop, The Pemberton Centre, 751 Ormskirk Road, Pemberton, Wigan, Lancashire, WN5 8AT

Cake Art Ltd, Unit 16, Crown Close, Crown Industrial Estate, Priorswood, Taunton, Somerset, TA2 8RX

Cynthia Venn, 3 Anker Lane, Stubbington, Fareham, Hants, PO14 3HF

Times Craft Centre Limited, 51 Mesnes Street, Wigan, Lancashire, WN1 1QX

Edited by Barbara Croxford
Designed by Sue Storey
Photography by David Gill

Published 1992 by Merehurst Limited
Ferry House
51–57 Lacy Road
Putney
London SW15 1PR

Copyright © Merehurst Limited 1992

A catalogue record for this book is available from the British Library
ISBN 1-85391-159-3

Typeset by Tradespools Ltd, Frome, Somerset
Colour separation by Fotographics, UK – Hong Kong
Printed by Leefung – Asco Printers Ltd, Hong Kong

CONTENTS

INTRODUCTION 7

EQUIPMENT 8

ABOUT ROYAL ICING 12

CAKE PREPARATION 22

COATING TECHNIQUES 30

LINEWORK 40

BORDER PIPING 46

CAKE DESIGN 56

TEXTURES AND EFFECTS 66

FLOWER PIPING 74

LETTERING 82

RUNOUT WORK 90

PRESSURE PIPING 100

STENCILLING 108

AIRBRUSHING 116

PAINTING 122

MODELLING 128

FINISHING TOUCHES 134

EXHIBITION WORK 140

TEMPLATES 148

INDEX 159

INTRODUCTION

For many years royal icing has been, and still is, a most popular medium for cake decoration. Although some people just make and decorate one-off cakes for special family celebrations or at Christmas, an increasing number are taking up this fascinating art form as a serious hobby or career. The endless possibilities and creative encouragement experienced while working with royal icing can lead to quite an obsession, it can become addictive – so be warned!

Many hobbyists turn their commitment to royal icing into a small but profitable home business making and decorating cakes, not forgetting those who continue with cake decoration as a career. *The Ultimate Book of Royal Icing* provides a clear and concise course covering every aspect of royal icing work, even experienced cake decorators and tutors will find this an invaluable source of instructive reference. My sixteen years experience as a lecturer and demonstrator in cake design and decoration, teaching to City & Guilds of London Institute standard, has given me the ability to set out the chapters in progressive stages of learning, in order to benefit both beginners and experienced alike. Also previously having worked in the celebration cake field of the confectionery industry has enabled me to pass on a great deal of the knowledge I gained over those many years to you the reader. Indeed I have not held anything back and all the so-called 'trade secrets' I have gleaned are here for you to use.

Writing this book has given me great pleasure and a sense of satisfaction, and I have realized an ambition made a number of years ago when my book *Confectionery Design* was published. My intention then was eventually to produce a practical but equally informative book to complement the theory of design set out in my first publication. At the outset I wanted to produce a book that would be both comprehensively instructive and inspirational. The first sections of the book deal with all the basic principles related to good royal icing work, the course then follows on with the skills of piping and coating. A well decorated cake relies on good design, a section devoted solely to cake design provides all the information you need to understand the basic elements of design, allowing you to eventually create your own original ideas. Linework piping,

lettering, runout work and pressure piping up to advanced level, lead on to the creative aspects of stencilling, airbrushing, modelling and useful advice on some finishing touches. Each section is detailed with colour photographs and easy to follow step-by-step instructions, with feature cakes that can be decorated once the skills of the particular section are mastered. The final part of the book, *Exhibition Work*, supposes an understanding of the skills introduced in the earlier sections of the book. It is unique in that it reveals many of the hints and tips used by professionals, not previously published.

Although there is a section on cake design, initially you may want to concentrate your time mastering the various elements of practical work such as coating, piping or even runout work, and then study the design aspect in more depth later. With this in mind and to enable you to start decorating immediately without having to sit down and first draw the feature cakes, the *Templates* section provides you with all the patterns, templates and outlines you will need. Tempting as it may be to do this, it is strongly advised that you at least glance through the pages of *Cake Design* and familiarize yourself with the various headings which in turn should, while you work on a royal icing project, remind you of the most important aspects that require attention to detail.

Apart from the traditional methods and styles which are an inevitable must in a specialist work such as this, I have studied hard to develop and perfect new techniques and feature numerous original ideas especially for this book. I am sure you will find it quite amazing, as I always do, what can be created from egg whites and icing sugar – the two ingredients used to make royal icing.

If you enjoy this book as much as I enjoyed putting it together, it should provide you with hours of pleasure, much encouragement and a source of inspiration for years to come.

Happy Royal Icing!

Lindsay

EQUIPMENT

Whether you are undertaking cake decoration as a career, a business or a hobby, you will need various tools and items of equipment. To make the work easier and more enjoyable, and to achieve better results, it is worthwhile obtaining the right equipment for the job. You do not necessarily need to rush out and buy everything, simply build up a collection of items as your interest and experience progresses. For example, you will always need to coat the cake in icing, so a turntable, palette knife, scraper and straight edge are the basics.

Study the following lists, decide on your needs, then shop around to find the best value, best quality and most useful equipment to buy.

A wide variety of turntables is available to suit every level of skill and indeed every pocket. Many plastic types can be purchased fairly inexpensively. However, keen enthusiasts and certainly professionals will easily justify the extra expense of one of the heavier and sturdier metal types or one with grip and tilt facility.

TOOLS AND EQUIPMENT FOR MARZIPANNING

ROLLING PIN
Select a good quality rolling pin, long enough for the largest cake you envisage making. Remember a large rolling pin can be used for smaller amounts of marzipan, but if you purchase one too small it may become redundant. The white polypropolene pins are an excellent buy. They are less likely to stick and certainly more hygienic than wooden rolling pins.

MARZIPAN SPACERS
A useful piece of equipment if you find difficulty in rolling an even thickness of marzipan. Simply place a spacer at each side of the marzipan you have started to roll, then rest the rolling pin on the spacers to achieve a perfectly even thickness (see page 27). The spacers can be used on opposite sides to give two variations of thickness.

MARZIPAN SMOOTHERS

Used extensively for sugarpaste work, these useful smoothers help achieve a superior finish to a marzipan covering. Remember the better the preparation the better the finish, smooth marzipan makes for a smoother coat of icing.

TOOLS AND EQUIPMENT FOR ROYAL ICING WORK

This is by no means the full range of tools and equipment that you will no doubt use as you progress and start to experiment with new techniques. However, it is a comprehensive list of items needed when commencing royal icing work. Many of the smaller items and sundries you will have in your kitchen already.

MEASURING JUG, WHISK AND SCALES

The basic ingredients of royal icing are egg albumen and icing (confectioner's) sugar. After reading *About Royal Icing*, you will appreciate that the reconstituted albumen powders have numerous advantages over fresh egg albumen (white). Therefore, you will need a measuring jug for water and a hand whisk (or a fork) to mix the powder into the water, with the scales for weighing the powder and icing sugar.

FINE MESH SIEVE

Many icing (confectioner's) sugars sold now contain a small percentage of calcium phosphate to improve the free running quality of the sugar. Provided you purchase your sugar from a shop or store with a quick turnover, the icing should be lump free, and for most everyday work may not need sieving. For competition work especially, or if your sugar is at all lumpy, sieve the sugar at least once maybe twice using a fine mesh sieve.

ELECTRIC FOOD MIXER

Royal icing can be mixed by hand, but for any large amounts it becomes a heavy mixture and is very tiring to mix, particularly to the correct consistency required. A good sturdy domestic food mixer (not a food processor) is invaluable if you intend making royal icing work a hobby.

TURNTABLES

These are made in various materials and designs from a very basic shallow plastic turntable, ideal for close work decoration on a finished cake, to the sturdy, heavy metal type. The main points to look for when purchasing a turntable is that the table is very free running so that rotating is easy and that there is a minimum of moving parts – the less there is, the less can go wrong.

Metal turntables are usually heavy and therefore sturdier and less prone to movement. Make sure the enamelling is good otherwise when cleaning it may flake off. Many of the plastic turntables are capable of holding large and heavy cakes. Test one out before you buy and read the specification on the box. Plastic turntables are lighter in weight and are easily cleaned after use. Many of them have the useful advantage of non-slip mats on the base and the table which ensures against movement.

For the serious cake decorator, turntables are readily available with lockable arms to grip the cake board and prevent movement, particularly useful when working on lightweight polystyrene dummies for exhibition and display work. Many also have an added tilting facility which is invaluable for making cake side decoration easier.

CAKE TILTER

If you do not have a tilting turntable, then a cake tilter to complement your standard turntable would be an advantage to make piping and decorating the sides of cakes easier. Many commercially available tilters are based on a hinged platform which is adjusted to the angle required. Some are made in stained wood, there are also laminated wood and plastic models. A less expensive option, but equally useful for small and medium size cakes, is a right angled metal tilter, at an angle of 45° degrees. It has a turned edge to hold the cake board in place.

SPOONS AND SPATULAS

You will need a selection of sizes of wooden spoons and plastic spatulas for various aspects of royal icing work.

PALETTE KNIVES

A good quality knife is a good investment. Ideally three knives in various sizes would make your work easier. But to start with buy the 18 cm (6 inch) bladed one. The next best buy would be a smaller 10 cm (4 inch) bladed knife. A small artist's palette knife is also very useful for delicate icing and in particular runout work. The plastic handled knives are usually dishwasher proof and probably more hygienic; but the feel and comfort in use of the traditional wooden handled knife cannot be equalled. Choose a knife with a firm yet slightly springy blade, not one that is thin and flimsy that bends easily.

CAKE SIDE SCRAPERS

Scrapers are available in plastic and stainless steel (see page 11). The steel ones are more rigid and will last longer if cleaned and stored carefully after use. Plastic ones are considerably less expensive but prone to scratching on the edge, resulting in lines in your icing when coating. Having said this, I always use good quality plastic scrapers for the slight flexibility, giving more control on awkward uneven cake sides. Provided you store them carefully they should last quite a while.

STRAIGHT EDGE

A good straight edge or metal rule is a worthwhile investment. Select a strong metal straight edge that will be sufficiently long enough for the width of the largest cakes you intend to ice. Most of the popular metal straight edges are made from anodized aluminium with polished edges to ensure a good finish to your icing. Available in various sizes, the most popular is the 40 cm (16 inch) length, however for large cakes a 45 cm (18 inch) edge is better.

PIPING TUBES (TIPS)

In most sugarcraft shops and icing specialist mail order catalogues, you will see various ranges of piping tubes (tips) with vastly differing prices. Yes you can buy very cheap piping tubes which will produce reasonably acceptable results; these cheaper tubes are mostly used by people who decorate just one-off cakes for the family or for their own enjoyment. The problem with some is that they have seams or overlaps in the metal which affect the shape of the icing as it is extruded from the tube. If you decide to use this type of cheaper tube, do look for the better quality ones.

The best tubes (tips) I prefer to use are the Bekenal or Supatube tubes. These are precision manufactured and, more importantly, are seamless so there is no break or overlap in the shape of the aperture. This is especially important in the finer writing tubes to enable the piping of perfect lines. Look after these tubes by cleaning, drying and storing carefully after use and they should last a lifetime.

Do not be tempted to buy the complete set of tubes (tips) offered in a particular range. Many of them you may never use, and some vary only slightly in design, so select the most useful to your needs. It is more economical to purchase tubes as you require them, for instance as your skill or interest in a particular technique develops. The basic set of tubes would probably consist of writing tubes No. 00, 0, 1, 2, 3 and 4, small star tubes No. 5, 6 and 7, large star tubes No. 11, 12, 13 and 15, and rope tubes No. 42, 43 and 44. A petal tube No. 58 and basket or ribbon tube No. 22 are useful additions.

PIPING BAG STAND

A most useful gadget that prevents the icing in the tube (tip) hardening and blocking the tube. Simply stand the filled piping bag through the holes in the top of the stand and the tip of the tube will be impressed into the moist foam sponge.

PIPING TUBE (TIP) CLEANING BRUSH

Rather than using good paint brushes and damaging the bristles or using a pointed metal implement, which damages the tube, to clean your tubes (tips), double-ended tube cleaners provide the ideal solution. Suitable for plain, star and shaped tubes.

The basis of good royal icing work must start with the right equipment for the job. Select quality items, care and maintain them and they should give a lifetime of service. Build up your requirements as and when your skills or interest in particular icing techniques develop.

SUNDRIES

SCISSORS
For general cutting of templates, ribbon, paper banding and piping bags etc.

PAINT BRUSHES
These are required for many aspects of cake decoration, such as neatening piped lines, painting food colours on icing and plaques, applying edible coloured petal dusting powder or even lifting a broken piped line off a cake! Keep a selection of small sable brushes and a few hair types.

PASTRY BRUSH
For application of boiled apricot jam to fruit cake before marzipanning (see page 26). A clean, dry pastry brush is also useful for cleaning icing dust from cake boards after removing take-off marks.

COCKTAIL STICKS (TOOTHPICKS)
Use the tips of cocktail sticks (toothpicks) for adding small dabs of colour to icing (see page 16). Other uses include supporting various icing work while drying. **Never** leave cocktail sticks in or on cakes.

FOAM SPONGE
Various shapes and sizes of foam sponge are useful for supporting icing work while drying. Small polystyrene blocks also offer the same useful purpose. Foam sponge is also used for stippling and texturing icing (see pages 73 and 137).

FLOWER OR ROSE NAILS
These are used as a rotating surface for piping all kinds of flowers. (See *Flower Piping*.)

ABOUT ROYAL ICING

Royal icing is a mixture of icing (confectioner's) sugar and egg white or albumen powder. It is used to coat cakes, in particular richly fruited ones covered with a layer of marzipan, to give a smooth or textured coating, and also to pipe decorations and inscriptions. In order to achieve good results with this fascinating and versatile icing, follow these few simple guidelines regarding selection of ingredients, preparation and mixing.

FRILL AND TULLE FLOWER CAKE

As a change to the conventional piped borders of shells, scrolls and bulbs, this cake features a piped frill made using special frilling tubes (tips) (see page 54). The fea- *ture decoration is provided by the delicate tulle flower in an attractive violet colour to tone with the delicate pink base colour (see page 129).*

INGREDIENTS

ICING (CONFECTIONER'S) SUGAR

Use a good quality icing (confectioner's) sugar purchased from a reputable store or sugarcraft shop. Beware of small boxes of sugar that have been on the shop shelves for any length of time and become lumpy or solid in a block through being near moisture. Most of the icing sugar available today is of excellent quality and some does contain a small percentage of calcium phosphate to assist its free running qualities.

If in any doubt sieve the icing sugar, it is better to spend a little extra preparation time than to encounter problems later when coating and piping. Always store icing sugar in a dry place, keeping the bag sealed.

For competition work (see *Exhibition Work*) where superior quality is paramount, select an extra fine Bridal Quality icing sugar.

ALBUMEN

As well as fresh egg albumen (white), there is now widely available a range of albumen powders, all of which are easy to use with no waste.

Pure Hen Albumen

Available in crystal and powder form, this albumen is the best quality and inevitably the most expensive. As the name pure implies, it does not contain any additives. It is recommended for runout work as it produces a strong icing.

To reconstitute the powder or crystals into liquid form, always follow the manufacturer's instructions which usually recommend:

Step 1

Measure 600 ml (1 pint/2½ cups) cold water into a clean greasefree bowl. Add and whisk in immediately 75 g (3 oz) pure hen albumen. The mixture will form a thick yellowy coloured mass on top with the water below; some mixture will adhere to the whisk, don't worry as this is quite normal. Leave the mixture to stand for 15 minutes (overnight in refrigerator for crystal type).

Royal icing is a mixture of two basic ingredients – icing sugar and albumen. Good quality icing sugar should be used with either pure albumen powder, albumen based powder or fresh egg whites.

1 Whisking albumen powder into the water.

2 Straining albumen solution ready for use.

Step 2

Re-whisk vigorously and the lumps will disperse. Strain the mixture through an extra fine sieve or mesh, then store in a clean container in the refrigerator. When required for making royal icing, remove from the refrigerator and allow it to come to room temperature for best results. The reconstituted mixture will keep for 4–5 days in the refrigerator.

Albumen Substitutes

These are considerably less expensive alternatives and far quicker to reconstitute with water. Use the same reconstitution technique as before; but this time as soon as you whisk the powder into the water it will disperse instantly and it is ready for use immediately. Albumen substitutes differ from pure hen albumen in that some contain additives to assist foaming qualities and stabilize the mixing. Acids, such as citric acid or acetic, are sometimes added to help the icing set and some contain starch or sugar as a filler. Used correctly, most of the powder products produce outstanding results and are widely used by cake decorators.

When making royal icing, these powders can be reconstituted in a different way, by sieving the powder with the dry icing (confectioner's) sugar, then adding the cold water before beating the mixture by hand or machine. It is acceptable, certainly if time is short, but I personally like to reconstitute the powder and add it to the icing sugar in liquid form. Using the sieving method with the pure hen albumen means that the soaking process is carried out in the actual icing mixture and if not dispersed sufficiently it will create lumps in the icing.

For a stronger royal icing to make runout pieces, the amount of albumen powder can be increased to 90 g (3½ oz) to each 600 ml (1 pint/2½ cups) water. I personally use the same basic quantities described previously for all royal icing work.

MAKING ROYAL ICING

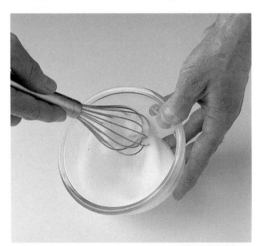

Whisking egg whites to a light foam.

Two recipes are given, one using fresh egg whites, the other using albumen powder or albumen based powder. Both recipes can be made by hand or machine. The hand-mixing method will take longer than the easier machine method. When mixing icing in a machine use the slowest speed.

Important Ensure that the bowl and all other equipment to be used are free of grease. Wash everything in hot soapy water, followed by a hot rinse. Allow the equipment to dry naturally or use a clean tea towel.

Right: Adding icing sugar to the egg whites.

Far Right: Making icing using an electric mixer.

Royal Icing using Fresh Egg Whites

about 2½ egg whites
450 g (1 lb/4 cups) icing (confectioner's)
sugar, finely sieved

Break up the egg whites in a bowl using a fork, then lightly whisk until frothy. Add about a quarter of the sieved sugar and mix well with a wooden spatula or spoon. Add the remaining sugar gradually, lightly mixing after each addition. Stir around the sides of the bowl to incorporate any dry sugar.

Continue lightly beating the mixture, either by hand or by machine until soft peaks are formed when the spatula or machine beater is lifted. Further beating will produce an icing of full peak consistency. Under-mixed icing will be heavy, glossy and slightly creamy in colour.
Note Depending upon the quantity of white in each egg, extra may be needed.

Royal Icing using Albumen Powder or Albumen Based Powder

12.5 g (½ oz) albumen powder or albu-
men based powder
90 ml (3 fl oz/⅓ cup) water
450 g (1 lb/4 cups) icing (confectioner's)
sugar, finely sieved

Depending upon the type of albumen powder used, prepare it according to the manufacturer's instructions or use the method on page 13. Strain the solution into a bowl.

Add half the sugar, mixing well with a wooden spatula or spoon. Add the remaining sugar and continue mixing until all the icing sugar is incorporated. Scrape down the sides of the bowl, then lightly beat the mixture by hand or machine until the desired peak (below) is achieved. The two main consistencies are known as soft and full peak.

PROFESSIONAL TIP
Using albumen powders eliminates the risk of infection from salmonella which may be present in raw egg whites.

ICING CONSISTENCY
There are two main terms that are used to describe the working consistency of royal icing.

Soft Peak
This is the first consistency reached during beating and is used for coating a cake. When lifted from the bowl with a spatula, the icing should retain a peak that will hold its shape but not be stiff and over-firm.

Full Peak
A stiffer, firmer consistency, leaving a definite bold peak when lifted from the bowl with a spatula. Use this icing for piping decorative borders that need to retain their shape as soon as they are piped. This consistency is also most suitable for runout work.

STORING ROYAL ICING
Store the prepared icing in an airtight container to prevent it from crusting over. For short term storage, simply cover the bowl of icing with a clean, damp cloth. Do not keep the icing in the refrigerator or freezer as it is neither necessary or beneficial to the keeping qualities.

Mixing the icing on slow speed.

Testing the peak consistency of the icing.

*Scraping down the sides
of the container.*

Always clean down the inside of the storage container after using the icing and before replacing the lid. Use a plastic spatula or wooden spoon for scraping down, particularly if the icing is in a plastic storage bowl. The action of a metal spoon scraping on a plastic bowl may remove thin slivers of plastic which could end up in the actual icing and in turn spoil a possibly good coating of icing. The plastic may also find its way into the piping tube (tip) and block it.

IMPROVERS

Glycerine

Glycerine is a hygroscopic liquid (attracts moisture) and will give the icing softer cutting and softer eating qualities. It can be purchased from sugarcraft shops and chemists. Simply add at the last stage of beating, 2.5 ml (½ teaspoon) glycerine for each 450 g (1 lb/4 cups) icing (confectioner's) sugar used. Do not add glycerine to icing for runout work.

Acid

Acid in the form of acetic, citric (lemon juice) or tartaric may be added to the icing at the beating stage. This helps to set the icing or strengthen it, for example when piping flowers, see *Flower Piping*.

COLOURINGS

A wider variety of colourings than ever before is now available. They come in liquid and paste form, powder and pens.

LIQUID COLOURS

Liquid colours are widely available and have been in use for many years. Use liquid colours for pastel tints. As they are less concentrated than paste colours, to achieve darker shades and deep colours like red, black and brown would require such a large amount: this would make the icing too soft to pipe with. Often bottles of liquid colour have a built-in dropper in the cap, making it particularly convenient to use.

PASTE COLOURS

Certain paste colours have been used professionally for a number of years, and are now commercially widely available in a comprehensive range of colours. They are regarded as the best to use for colouring royal icing. Use the tip of a cocktail stick (toothpick) to add the colour in small amounts until the desired tint or shade is produced.

The only disadvantage with paste colours occurs when you make runout pieces with very dark coloured icing. The amount of glycerine in the colour could affect the drying time and the resultant texture may be crumbly. To avoid this, instead paint dry light coloured runouts with darker colours, see page 133. Alternatively, there are colours available containing no glycerine, but the colour range is very limited.

*Carefully adding colour
to the icing.*

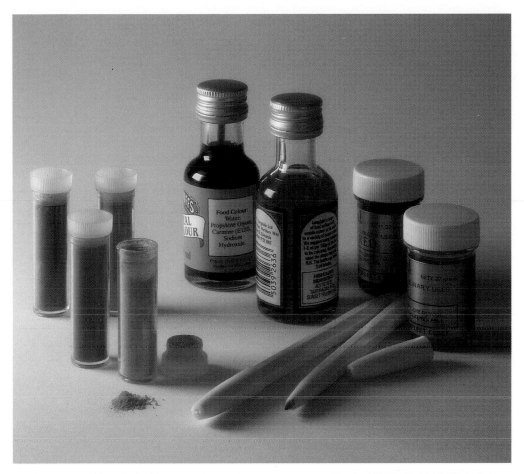

A variety of food colourings each with their own particular characteristics is available for colouring royal icing. Each type has advantages for different applications. Those available include liquid, paste, powder and food colour pens.

POWDER COLOURS

This type is mainly used for dusting the centres or petal edges of flowers and the edge of frills. It can be used to colour icing, but as the intensity is not very strong it is uneconomical to use in large quantities. Because paste colours contain glycerine, it is advisable to use powder colour in royal icing intended for piping lace and filigree work, as it produces a much stronger setting icing.

COLOUR PENS

Sugarcraft pens are a most useful aid to quick decoration and for fine outlining and intricate detail. They are used just like felt tip pens but the colour is edible. For some people, especially novice cake decorators, these pens make writing on a cake much easier than piping! (See page 125.)

COLOUR MIXING

Although there is a wide range of colours available to produce beautifully attractive tints and shades, these colours can be mixed to provide even better colours. Just as a painter artist would not use colours straight from the tube, the sugarcraft artist should blend and experiment with edible paste colours. Try these examples for a start and then make notes of your own special colour combinations. Empty paste colour jars can be used to store large amounts of mixed colour, putting your own colour label on them. The various uses of colour in designing your own cakes is described fully in *Cake Design*.

The following ideas can be blended in the actual icing.

GREEN

To improve upon the basic green colours available, a much better looking green can be made by adding a small amount of yellow to produce either a leaf green or pistachio green, or with tangerine a more 'earthy' green colour for foliage. These additions make the green less of a mint colour.

CREAM

Use a very small amount of tangerine colour to obtain an attractive cream tint. You can dull the colour a little with a touch of brown or chestnut.

VIOLET

Improve upon the violet colours available by adding either more pink or more blue to achieve the required pinky-violet or blue-violet.

RED

Strong Christmas red colour is widely available in a conventional type paste and a thicker more concentrated paste, the colour intensity of which improves after allowing the icing to stand for about 30 minutes. To make a brighter red, add a small amount of tangerine colour, this really works!

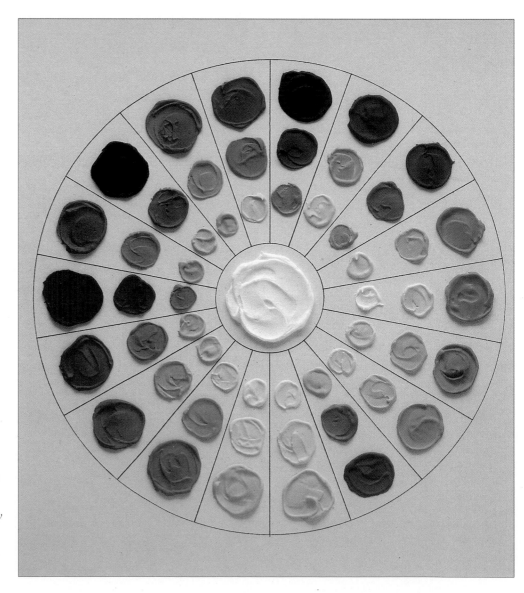

Most types of colourings offer a good range, especially paste colours as shown here. From the eighteen colours available, numerous hues can be produced by varying the amount added to the icing to make light tints through to full strength colours.

MIXING COLOURED ICING

From the already extensive range of colours of icing shown on the chart opposite, even more colours both subtle and striking can be achieved by very careful mixing and blending as shown below. This is by no means a complete range and further experimenting will prove quite rewarding.

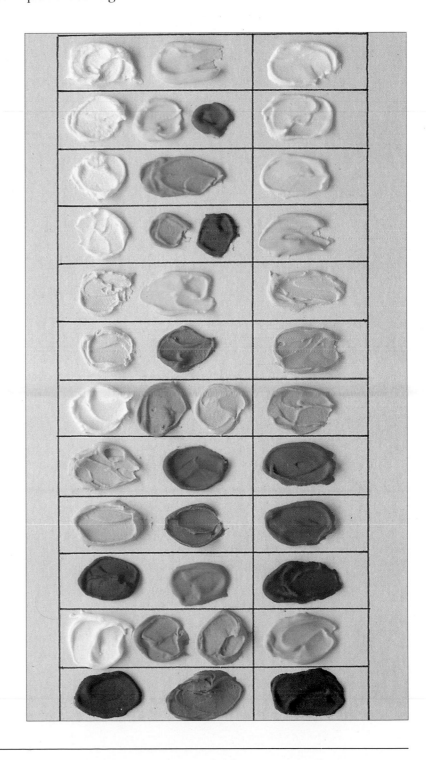

WHITE + LEMON = OFF WHITE

WHITE + LEMON + BROWN = IVORY

WHITE + TANGERINE = CREAM

WHITE + TANGERINE + BROWN = BISCUIT

MINT GREEN + YELLOW = PISTACHIO

MINT GREEN + DARK BLUE = EMERALD

WHITE + TANGERINE + GREEN = COFFEE

VIOLET + PINK = CLARET

VIOLET + DARK BLUE = PURPLE

RED + TANGERINE = BRIGHT RED

WHITE + PINK + TANGERINE = SKINTONE

DARK BROWN + DARK BLUE = BLACK

MAKING A PIPING BAG

For good results with your piping, start with well made piping bags made from quality greaseproof (waxed) paper. They are much easier to control than plastic bags or metal icing syringes.

Piping bags should not be made too large for such a stiff medium as royal icing, otherwise the pressure required to force the icing out may burst the bag. The rule to remember is the smaller the tube (tip) the smaller the bag. So for tubes from No. 000 to No. 4 use small bags, larger plain tubes and small star and rope tubes are best in medium bags. Large rope, star, basket and petal tubes could be used in slightly larger bags.

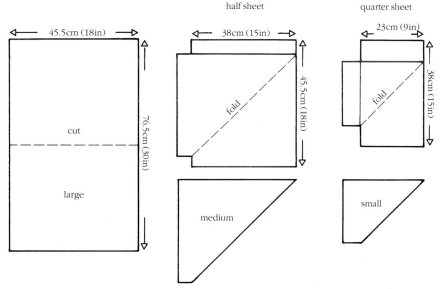

Before commencing piping, try to estimate how many bags you will use and make them ready. If using various colours and different tubes, you will need several bags for each one.

There are different methods for making piping bags; I recommend you choose the one which you find most comfortable. If you can already make bags, then do not change if you are happy with them. The method shown here is quite easy to follow and produces secure bags of a good shape.

Step 1

Select the paper size as required. Fold the paper diagonally to produce a right angle at the corner as shown; the corners should not meet exactly. Cut along the fold to make two triangles.

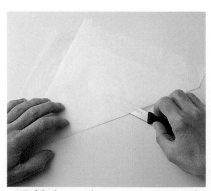

1 Folded paper being cut into triangles.

2 Holding paper to form cone shape.

3 Bringing left-hand point over.

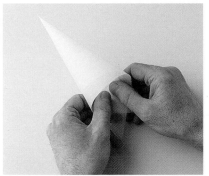

4 Positioning all three points together.

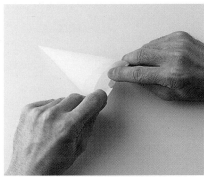

5 Folding over and tucking in.

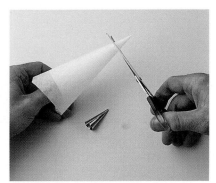

6 Cutting end off bag to fit tube.

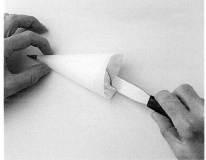

7 Using a small knife to add the icing.

8 Folding the top over twice.

9 The piping bag placed in a stand.

Step 2

Hold the triangle with the point of the right angle facing you and fold the corner inwards. Bring the curving corner over and make it meet the point of the right angle.

Step 3

With the other hand bring the left-hand point over, around the back of the cone and under to meet the point of the right angle at the back.

Step 4

Hold all the points with the fingers of one hand as shown, and slide the front point and back point up or down to tighten the point of the bag.

Step 5

Fold all three points inside the bag. Make a small tear in the centre of the folds, folding one side over to lock all points securely together.

Step 6

Having selected the tube (tip) to use, neatly cut off the end of the bag with scissors and insert the tube. As a guide have two-thirds of the tube inside the bag and one third protruding.

Step 7

Hold the bag in one hand and fill the bag about two-thirds full with the icing. Hold the top of the bag firmly against the palette knife and gently pull out the knife. Fold the points of the bag inwards.

Step 8

Fold the top of the bag over twice. This seals the top and, providing the bag is held and squeezed correctly, the icing will remain in the bag and not be forced out at the top.

Step 9

To stop the icing hardening in the end of the tube (tip), place the prepared piping bag in a piping bag stand. The moist sponge at the base prevents the tube becoming clogged with hard icing.

Alternatively, cut a slit in a piece of foam sponge, moisten the sponge and rest the bag on the table with the tip of the tube in the slit.

CAKE PREPARATION

Royal icing is used for coating cakes and decorating them. For decoration it is used on rich fruit cakes, medium and lightly fruited cakes and also on sponge and genoese cakes, whether covered in royal icing or sugarpaste. Royal icing can also decorate chocolate work and buttercream cakes.

For coating, royal icing is normally used only on fruit cakes because the icing sets very firmly and therefore needs a sufficiently strong enough base to support it – a fruit cake with its covering of marzipan is ideal. However, there may be occasions when you will be required to coat a sponge based cake with royal icing, perhaps for a wedding where the bride or guests prefer a lighter cake or for someone who dislikes fruit cake. Providing the cake is covered with either marzipan or sugarpaste, prior to coating with royal icing, the cake is well supported on a cake stand or, if necessary, with special dowel support cake pillars, there should not be any problems.

Cutting qualities play an important part of a well made cake. When cutting a soft sponge cake coated with hard royal icing, the icing could crack and the cake collapse under the pressure of the knife. To avoid this, use one of the new improvers or additives which can be incorporated into the icing mixture to make a softer setting icing. This has the effect of adding glycerine to the icing.

With fruit cakes, cutting qualities are ideal. The cake is firm, the marzipan is firm (not hard) and icing is firm, this enables the cake as a whole to be cut into neat slices. Obviously the success of a good cutting cake does depend on a good quality fruit cake.

IMPROVING THE CAKE

Having made the fruit cake, you will need to store it for a few weeks or months to mature. This maturing process helps improve the cake both in texture and flavour. During the process, the sugars and fruit sugar play a part in developing the texture and improving the flavour. Any harshness or bitterness in the flavour, familiar in a cake eaten soon after baking, is removed and the cake develops a pleasant mellow flavour.

The first stage in improving the cake is the addition of spirit a short while after the cake leaves the oven. I like to apply the first addition about 30 minutes after baking is complete and while the cake is still warm. This has the effect of closing the 'crumb' or texture of the cake and penetrating more evenly through the cake than if it was cold.

STORING

Store the cake in a material that will let it breath, such as greaseproof (waxed) paper, loosely overwrapped with a polythene bag. Take care when using polythene, only loosely wrap. Foil is suitable if a barrier (such as greaseproof or waxed paper) between the foil and the cake is provided. Foil in direct contact can cause metal contamination to the cake. It is also advisable to label the cake with the date of baking.

When storing the cake, leave the greaseproof paper used to line the cake tin intact on the cake. This will provide protection to the cake during handling, assist in preventing it drying out and make the addition of spirit easier.

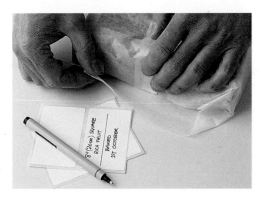

Wrapping and labelling ready for storage.

ORANGE ROSE WEDDING CAKE

A most unusual idea for a cake, the tiers are simply round cakes cut in half, then marzipanned and iced in the conventional manner. The simple decoration consists only of linework, filigree and roses made by overlaying runout sections on top of each other to give a sense of depth to the flower. (See Templates.)

ADDING SPIRIT

Improving the texture can be aided by the addition of spirit, such as rum or

Brushing spirit on to the fruit cake.

brandy. These are the two spirits I use and would recommend as providing the most beneficial flavour to complement a rich fruit cake.

During the storage or maturing time, unwrap the cake and liberally apply the spirit over the cake using a pastry brush. Allow the spirit to soak in and then wrap the cake, storing for a few more weeks. You may like to add spirit two or three times during the maturing process, which can be anything from one to three months. The final addition of spirit can be made prior to marzipanning as shown. Experience will tell you how much or how little extra moisture is required.

LEVELLING THE CAKE

Sometimes you may make or be given a cake for coating which has a peaked top or a hollow in the centre. Just a little pre-preparation before marzipanning will make the job easier and more accurate.

PEAKED TOP

There are two choices to remedy this problem. Either cut off the peak so that the cake is level – some people do not like doing this because it seems a waste, but you can use the trimmings for rum truffles. The alternative is to make a hollow in the rolled out marzipan top if the peak is not too pointed, if it is you will definitely have to trim at least a little off.

Levelling off the top of a peaked cake.

HOLLOW TOP

For this problem, brush the hollow with prepared apricot jam. Shape an extra piece of marzipan, thick in the middle and thinner at the edges to sit neatly in the hollow, then lightly flatten with a rolling pin. The cake is then ready for marzipanning.

Pressing marzipan into a hollow cake top.

PROFESSIONAL TIP
Cut one of your cakes every so often to test the eating quality for yourself – after all it is no use continually decorating fruit cakes that don't taste good!

GENERAL PREPARATION

Even if you have made a cake with a good level top, you will no doubt find that when you remove the greaseproof (waxed) paper before marzipanning that small lumps of cake or fruit pull away with the paper, especially at the corners of a square cake. So before marzipanning, check the cake and fill any holes and corners with small 'plugs' of marzipan, sticking them in position with a little apricot glaze.

Plugging small holes with marzipan.

COVERING THE CAKE WITH MARZIPAN

Marzipan is basically a paste mixture made from nibbed (slivered) almonds and sugar, the proportion of almonds to sugar varies according to the quality of paste and the manufacturer. Sometimes commercial marzipans contain a proportion of ground apricot kernels or peach kernels and occasionally ground soya beans or soy flour. Egg white or whole egg is sometimes added.

Varying types are available but the two most popular are white and yellow marzipan. The main difference is the colour which is a matter of personal preference.

As mentioned in *Coating Techniques*, most royal iced cakes require a crisp right angled edge especially for runout collars or designs where the coated top edge is integrated as part of the design. An accurate coating of icing relies upon good preparation of the marzipan covering. Using the following method should give very satisfactory results.

As the marzipan is very easy to work with, to cover the top and sides of a cake is a fairly simple technique.

When rolling out marzipan you will need icing (confectioner's) sugar for dusting, to prevent the marzipan sticking to the work surface. An icing sugar dredger is a handy piece of equipment to store the sugar and makes working easier and cleaner.

Note Remember as always with any food work to provide a clean working environment, ensuring that work surfaces are clean and all equipment is clean ready for use. Before commencing the work, wash your hands and clean your fingernails thoroughly.

APRICOT GLAZE

To stick marzipan to the cake it is best to use a neutral flavoured and coloured jam, such as apricot jam. For example, using lemon curd with its pronounced flavour or deeply coloured raspberry jam should be avoided. The jam should be boiled immediately prior to use, to sterilize it and reduce the risk of mould forming between the cake and the marzipan. Boiling the jam also encourages a better

Marzipan is readily available in two main types; natural (white) and golden (yellow). Both are obtainable in the same quality low or high almond contents.

adhesion than using it cold. Bring the jam to the boil in a saucepan or use the microwave to heat the jam in a suitable container. A pastry brush is required to apply the jam to the fruit cake. (Further reading on choice of equipment can be found in *Equipment*.)

Apricot Glaze

450 g (1 lb) apricot jam (jelly)
30 ml (2 tablespoons) water

Place the jam and water in a saucepan (or suitable dish for microwave). Heat until the jam has melted and bring to the boil. Alternatively, microwave according to manufacturer's instructions. Strain the mixture through a sieve, discarding the fruit pulp and skins that remain, then use.

CALCULATING THE MARZIPAN REQUIRED

The easiest and simplest method of calculating the amount of marzipan required, without the need for long charts and tables, is to weigh the baked

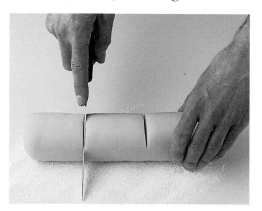

Cutting proportions for top and sides.

Half of the total weight of fruit cake will determine weight of marzipan, then divide into thirds.

Two-thirds of the marzipan will cover the top of the cake, the remaining one third will be sufficient to cover the sides of the cake.

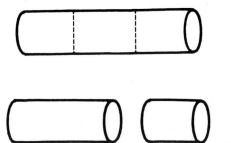

cake (it will be slightly lighter than before baking) and divide the weight by two, providing the amount of marzipan required to cover the top and sides.

When you commence covering the cake, roughly shape the marzipan into a large roll. Mark the roll into thirds and cut off one third. This is for the sides and the larger two-thirds is for the top. This calculation gives a good average covering, if you like more or less marzipan, adjust accordingly.

WARMING MARZIPAN

Before using, it is best (usually on the manufacturer's instructions) to warm the marzipan, then lightly knead to make it pliable and easier to roll. To warm marzipan, place it on a piece of greaseproof (waxed) paper on a baking sheet in a very low oven for a few minutes. Alternatively, place the marzipan on a suitable plate and microwave for a few seconds only.

Do not use marzipan if it has been in a cold place and it is hard. Trying to knead and roll it in this state will result in severe oiling, which in turn will spoil the subsequent coating of royal icing.

COVERING ROUND CAKES

Step 1
Brush the cake top with apricot glaze (see Professional Tip).

Step 2
Roll out the portion of marzipan for the top of the cake into a neat circular shape, just a fraction larger than the diameter of the cake top. If you have a cake with a

1 Brushing the cake with apricot glaze.

peaked top (see Levelling the Cake) that you do not want to cut off, then impress a shallow hollow to accommodate the uneven shape. Position the cake on the marzipan. Press well down on the cake top taking care not to break the cake. Push your fingers around the edge as shown to force the marzipan up to the cake – with a perfectly level cake or one that is being marzipanned upside down (using the base as the top!) this will not be necessary. Trim away any excess marzipan.

2 Firming the marzipan to the cake top edge.

Step 3

Take the remaining marzipan and providing the trimmings from the top are clean (remove any cake crumbs!), knead together. Roll out in a long sausage shape, then press down along the length with your knuckles. Roll flat, using marzipan spacers if liked, increasing the width to just slightly larger than the depth of the cake side.

3 Using spacers to roll accurate thickness.

Step 4

To obtain the required length, measure the cake circumference with a piece of string. Alternatively, put a mark at one end of the marzipan and on the cake top. Align the marks, then carefully roll the cake along the surface. When the mark reaches the surface again, the circumference will be measured. Mark the marzipan about 1.5 cm (½ inch) longer for an overlap. Trim to neaten one long edge and one short edge, then roll up the marzipan Swiss roll fashion, starting at the uncut shorter edge. Brush the cake side with apricot glaze.

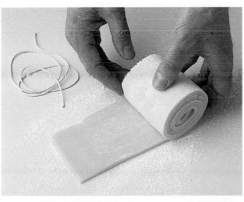

4 Rolling the marzipan 'Swiss roll' fashion.

Step 5

Making sure the cut edge is on the work surface, unravel the marzipan around the cake side. Where the marzipan overlaps, cut through with a knife and bond the two cut edges together. Again using a knife, trim off the excess marzipan from the top edge, moving the blade towards the centre as you cut around the edge. Press the marzipan firmly on to the cake side using smoothers. Place the cake on a board at least 5 cm (2 inches), and preferably 7.5 cm (3 inches), larger than the cake.

5 Unravelling marzipan around the cake side.

COVERING SQUARE CAKES

Step 1

For the top of the cake use the same method as for round cakes, but roll out the marzipan into a square shape and position the cake on top.

Step 2

For the sides, roll out a large rectangular shape of marzipan to measure just slightly larger than the width of the cake side and four times the depth of the cake side. Trim the edges to neaten.

Brush the sides of the cake with apricot glaze. Hold the cake as shown with the top edge of the marzipanned cake level with the cut edge of the rolled out marzipan.

Step 3

A good level cake should stand on its own long enough for you to trim around accurately.

1 Marzipanning top of square cake.

2 Positioning for the first side.

3 Trimming marzipan along the base.

4 Positioning for the second side.

Step 4
Lift the cake and rotate to the next side and repeat the process. Continue until each side is covered. Neaten the work with marzipan smoothers, then place the cake on a board (about 5–7.5 cm (2–3 inches) wider than the cake.

COVERING LARGE CAKES
For large cakes, or if you find the previous method difficult, roll out the marzipan as before but cut into four rectangles each the size of the cake sides – use string or a ruler to measure the cake. To apply the prepared pieces, lift them on to the cake side as shown, use smoothers to obtain a perfect finish.

COVERING SHAPED CAKES
The tops of most shaped cakes, such as petal, heart and hexagonal, can be

Attaching separate marzipan rectangles.

marzipanned using the method for round cakes. For the sides use the round cake method for cakes without corners, like oval, heart and petal; for cakes with corners, such as oblong, octagonal and triangular, use the square cake method.

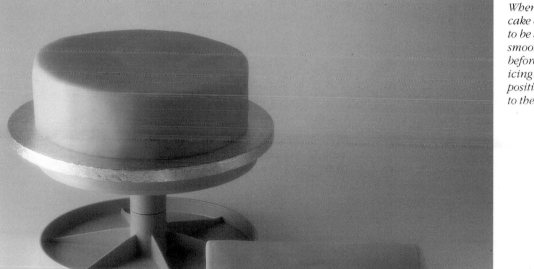

PROFESSIONAL TIP
When marzipanning cake corners, they need to be accurately smoothed and formed before coating with royal icing. Use two scrapers positioned at right angles to the corner.

Once marzipanned the finished cakes can be transferred on to cake boards as shown and allowed to firm for 24 hours before the first coat of royal icing is applied. The choice of either natural or golden marzipan will depend on your own or the recipient's personal taste.

COATING TECHNIQUES

Having covered your cake with marzipan, allow the marzipan to firm up for about 24 hours prior to coating the cake. You are now ready to coat the cake with royal icing in preparation for decorating.

Make up the royal icing, beating to 'soft peak' consistency (see page 15). If the icing is overbeaten and too firm, it will contain many air bubbles which will appear on the cake surface, also the icing will dry very hard and brittle. If the icing is underbeaten, it will be heavy and 'wet', taking a long time to dry which can create problems.

Get yourself organized ready for coating so that everything is to hand. You will need the prepared royal icing, turntable, spatula or wooden spoon, palette knife, straight edge and side scraper. You will also require a clean, damp cloth to keep the work area clean.

The turntable and cake must be steady so that coating is easier and more accurate. Many of the new turntables available have a non-slip mat on the top to steady the cake and on the base to steady the turntable itself. If you have a turntable without this facility, the best way to adapt it is to put a clean, damp cloth or square sponge cloth on the top and one underneath the turntable. Make sure the cloths are even, not folded or doubled unevenly.

ADJUSTING THE CONSISTENCY

Having made the icing, remove sufficient to coat the cake and place into a clean bowl, covering with a clean moist cloth to prevent crusting. Next adjust the consistency of the icing ready for coating by adding a few drops of cold water. Stir the

Adding water to adjust the consistency of the icing.

water gently into the icing, this will help disperse the air bubbles. DO NOT beat the water into the icing, this will incorporate more air bubbles.

Many text books recommend leaving icing to stand. This is unnecessary, providing the icing consistency is adjusted, you can work with it immediately.

PROFESSIONAL TIP
Many people believe that over-handling is the main cause of marzipan staining the icing on a cake. In fact the icing consistency has a great deal to do with the avoidance of this problem. If the icing is heavy, wet and glossy in appearance, it is most likely underbeaten. Using icing of this nature, particularly for a first coat, means that the drying time is extended. This results in the moist icing drawing the oil from the marzipan causing staining on the icing.
Use freshly beaten icing thinly for the first coat to encourage rapid drying.

COLOUR ADDITION

Colour may be added to the icing at this stage. Use a good quality paste or liquid food colouring (see page 16). For liquid colour use a dropper to add the colour in small amounts. Paste colour can be added to icing using the tip of a cocktail stick (toothpick). Add sufficient colour to make the desired tint or shade.

When decorating a number of cakes that need to be matching in colour, such as a multi-tiered wedding cake, it is advisable to mix sufficient coloured icing at this stage. Trying to achieve an exact colour match if the icing supply is exhausted can be quite difficult and sometimes impossible, particularly if the colour is a combination of two or more colours. If using liquid colours there is less of a problem if you run short of icing. When mixing the first batch of coloured icing, weigh the amount of icing and count the number of drops of colour added. Make a note of the formula and keep it safe, ready to mix another batch with an exact colour match.

Mixing in colour until completely blended.

SIDE COATING ROUND CAKES

Place the cake centrally on the turntable and start to apply icing to the cake side. Hold the palette knife vertically and position your finger at the back of the blade as shown to apply pressure to the icing and so disperse any remaining air bubbles. Start to rotate the turntable with your other hand and paddle the icing as you work to form a neat, relatively smooth and even thickness of icing. Ensure that the icing completely covers the sides from top to bottom and that no marzipan can be seen.

Initially use a traditional plain cake side scraper to create a smooth even coating. Position the side scraper almost resting on the cake board, holding towards you at an angle of about 15 degrees. With the other hand, slowly (but not too slowly otherwise ridges appear in

the icing) rotate the turntable in one continuous movement all the way round, then pull the scraper off towards yourself. At this stage you will have a vertical line down the cake side, this is known as the 'take off' mark and is removed as the coating process continues. Take-off marks are discussed on page 34.

PROFESSIONAL TIP
Each time you finish using and before you put down your knife, straight edge or side scraper during the coating process, take time to remove any excess icing and return it to the bowl (providing it has not crusted over). Wipe the piece of equipment clean ready for using again – it takes only minutes but saves a lot of time in the long run. Far easier to clean off soft icing than hard icing!

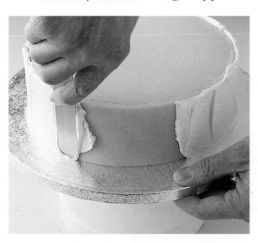

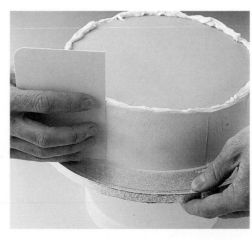

Far Left: Paddling icing around the cake side.

Left: Smoothing the icing using a side scraper.

TIDYING THE TOP EDGE

Before setting the cake aside to dry, the top edge must be neatened, otherwise the uneven band of icing around the edge will dry and subsequent coats will be difficult to work. Hold the palette knife horizontally on the cake top and rotate the turntable slowly, at the same time moving the knife into the centre of the cake to neatly remove the icing. Stop about two or three times to clean off the knife so that a build up of icing does not occur. DO NOT pull the knife outwards from the cake, as this will result in an uneven band of icing at the top edge.

Trimming excess icing from the top edge.

CLEANING THE CAKE BOARD

Before leaving the icing to dry, ensure that the cake board is clean and free from unwanted icing by removing it with a palette knife. To coat a cake and leave the board untidy creates a problem when adding the next coat of icing. The icing left on the board will have set hard and make good coating difficult if not impossible.

Cleaning excess icing from the cake board.

SIDE COATING SQUARE CAKES

The principle is the same as for round cakes, except that there are four corners to contend with. Apply the icing in the same way and start the first side as for the round cake, positioning the scraper at an angle. With the other hand keep the turntable still, then move the scraper along the cake side slowly but smoothly, keeping it steady as you work. At the end of the side, pull the scraper off towards yourself as for the round cake take-off. Remove any excess icing on the scraper and commence with the second side, starting by bringing the take-off mark from the previous side round and on to the second side. Repeat the side coating technique as for the first side and

Smoothing the sides of a square cake.

continue around the cake until all four sides are coated.

PROFESSIONAL TIP
Preference for coating the top or the side of the cake first is purely a matter of personal choice. There are no hard and fast rules. The reason I always coat the sides first is that the icing bonds the cake to the board and stops it from moving around when coating the top. Cake movement is not much of a problem when you are icing a rich fruit cake, as normally the heavy weight of cake and marzipan prevents any movement. The matter is quite different though when coating lightweight polystyrene cake dummies for display work. There are various methods of securing the dummy to the cake board (see Exhibition Work) but this simple method of coating the side first is an easy and reliable option.

DRYING ICING BETWEEN COATS

It is important to allow the icing to dry between coats, so that a sound surface is achieved in preparation for subsequent coats. However, do not let the icing dry rock hard as this will prevent a good adhesion being formed with each new layer of soft icing. As a result when the cake is cut, the icing will shatter and splinter in shreds as opposed to cutting cleanly.

Drying times vary with conditions, as a rule the icing should sound dry when lightly tapped with a finger. It is best to leave icing overnight in a warm, dry atmosphere.

TOP COATING ROUND AND SQUARE CAKES

Using similar techniques of application, paddling, applying pressure and rotating the turntable, prepare the cake top with a fairly smooth and even thickness of royal icing. Hold the palette knife horizontally to the cake top as shown.

Remove the cake from the turntable and place it on the work surface. It is advisable to put a moist cloth or non slip mat beneath the cake board to prevent the cake moving during coating – ensure that the cloth or mat is even and not folded.

Take the clean straight edge and, holding firmly at each end, position it at an angle of about 45 degrees to the surface at the edge farthest away from yourself. Draw it across the cake in one continuous movement, on reaching the edge nearest to yourself keep the straight edge at the same level and pull away fairly rapidly.

If the icing has lines or air bubbles in it, immediately place the straight edge on the icing and repeat the technique, this time applying a little more pressure to disperse the air bubbles and lines. If you remember the areas which were unsatisfactory on the previous coat, it is easier to remedy. For instance you may have had lines on the right hand side, so on the next coat apply a similar pressure to the

Paddling icing using a circular motion.

Smoothing the top using a straight edge.

icing on the left side because that was sufficiently smooth, but apply more pressure on the right side.

Trimming the top edge using a palette knife.

Many tutors and text books will advise you to push the straight edge backwards and forwards in the icing to smooth it out, when really in effect you are aerating it (incorporating more air bubbles) which is exactly what you don't want to do! Never do this.

As with the side coating, ensure that the top edges are neat before setting the cake aside to dry. This time hold the knife vertically against the cake side and move the blade down as you rotate the turntable. Clean the knife off two or three times as you work. Make absolutely sure that there are no soft icing lumps remaining on the dry side coat because when these dry they can make subsequent side coating very difficult.

TAKE-OFF MARKS

Unsightly take-off marks can be reduced to a minimum by using slightly softer consistency of icing for each subsequent coat, and by making each coat thinner towards the final coat by taking off more icing with the side scraper. Take-off marks should be removed only when the

Removing the take-off mark with a knife.

icing is dry and before each subsequent coat. Use a small bladed sharp knife to shave off the icing in shreds, when the cake feels smooth to the touch (use a clean, dry hand to test) the cake is ready for its next coat. Clean the icing dust from the board using a soft bristled pastry brush.

Never scrape off the take-off mark from the last coat as the area will become more, instead of less noticeable, especially if coloured icing is used. The scraped area will be lighter than the coated area.

Throughout the book, various ways of camouflaging take-off marks can be seen (see pages 143 and 144). Usually a side decoration or linework piping disguises them. As a rule the mark is concealed at the back of the cake so that when the cake is displayed the take-off mark is not noticeable.

SECOND AND SUBSEQUENT COATS

Having mastered the technique of coating the top and the sides of cakes separately, you can now proceed with the second coat of icing. Use the same techniques for coating the side, allowing it to dry, then coating the top and allowing that to dry. A third coating of icing is normally sufficient. However, for competition and display work (see *Exhibition Work*) more coats are usually applied to produce a superior finish to the icing. Use a slightly softer consistency of royal icing for each subsequent coat of icing.

COATING SHAPED CAKES

Most shaped cakes can be coated using the conventional method described for round or square cakes.

Always aim to finish with the take-off mark at the 'back' of the cake, for instance an oval shaped cake would be finished at the centre of a long side. It does not make much difference whether you start with the side coating or the top. Practice for yourself to achieve the method and result you are happy with.

A brief description of how to adapt the basic technique for each shape is given below:

OBLONG
Use the same technique described for square cakes. The only difference is that two sides are longer – this does not affect the technique in any way.

Smoothing the sides of an oblong cake.

OCTAGONAL AND HEXAGONAL
Coat as for square cakes but coat alternate sides, allowing them to dry before coating adjacent sides. As a rule, coat a side, miss a side. Allow to dry, then coat the uncoated side and leave the coated side. Repeat the method until the desired quality of coating is achieved.

Icing alternate sides of a hexagonal cake.

TRIANGULAR
For a triangular shaped cake, commence smoothing with the straight edge held at the point rather than a straight side. Coat as for square cakes but treat each separate face of the triangle as a cake side, coating alternately as for the octagon and hexagon shape.

Smoothing the top of a triangular cake.

Finishing at the centre of a long oval side.

OVAL

Coat as for round cakes taking care to move the scraper out to follow the widening shape of the oval.

Smoothing the two sides of a heart cake.

HEART AND PETAL

Start in the crevice of a heart and each crevice of a petal shape, moving the scraper carefully round the shape as you rotate the turntable. For a petal shape coat alternate petals as for the octagon and hexagon shaped cakes, allowing the icing to dry before coating adjacent sides. For a heart shape, treat the right and left of the heart as separate sides.

Applying icing to a horseshoe cake.

HORSESHOE

Coat the outer curved side as for a round cake. For the inside curve, use a palette knife in a vertical position to smooth round in one complete movement. The two flat ends can be treated as for the sides of a square cake. Coat the inside, outside and ends separately.

CUT SCRAPERS

The plain cake side scraper used to give a completely smooth finish to the icing is the most popular. However, there are many interesting shapes, patterns and effects to be achieved by using cut scrapers. These scrapers are all the same size and basic shape except that the straight edge used to obtain a smooth side is cut with various configurations. They can be used on cakes of any shape and produce some spectacular results which are achieved so easily.

Cut scrapers should only be used on the final coating of the cake side, as obviously it would be quite difficult to re-align the configurations accurately each time you apply a coat. Try experimenting with these scrapers, there is no extra skill involved, it is simply a matter of replacing the plain scraper with a cut scraper.

COMB SCRAPER

This scraper produces a series of horizontally grooved lines around the cake side.

Available from sugarcraft shops in plastic and metal; use them to produce an interesting line effect.

SINGLE LINE SCRAPER

This scraper gives the illusion of a line that has been accurately piped directly on the cake side. Paper banding or ribbon looks good above the line.

Using a sharp craft knife or small metal file, shape a cut-out in a conventional plastic scraper to produce the effect of a piped line.

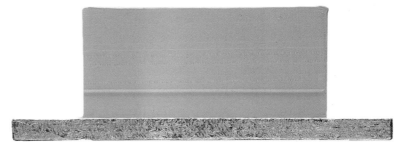

TRIPLE LINE SCRAPER

These lines are located closer together and are graduated to give the appearance of No. 3, 2 and 1 lines.

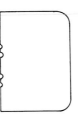

The same principle as described above can be used to produce a more detailed combination of line widths. Use space between the lines for ribbon.

DOUBLE LINE AND CURVE SCRAPER

This scraper makes an interesting combination of pattern that can be further enhanced with linework and other decoration.

A group of three lines quite close together makes a neat design for a cake side. For extra effect, add a fine scallop pattern piped adjacent to the outer line.

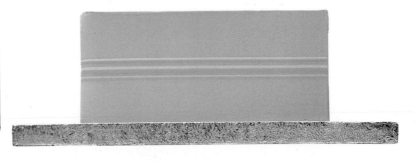

QUICK COATING

For some commercial outlets and indeed for yourself if time is short, coating the top and sides of the cake in one operation can be a time-saving advantage, instead of coating the top and side separately.

Many cake decorators always use this method for a first coat to cover the cake all over, then return to the traditional top and side method for subsequent coats. If carried out neatly and fairly accurately, this technique can be used to simply coat the cake three times. However, it is only really suitable if you intend to apply a piped border which will conceal the angular top edge. For competition work and general work where runout collars are to be incorporated, it is far better to produce a crisp, accurate and right angled edge using the traditional method.

Apply the icing as described earlier, but cover the cake top and sides completely using just the palette knife.

Applying the icing to completely cover the cake.

Right: Smoothing the cake side with a scraper.

Far Right: Neatly bevelling the top edge at an angle.

Smooth the top using the straight edge. Hold the palette knife at an angle as shown, with the other hand rotate the turntable. Remove any excess icing from the top edge.

Now use the side scraper as described earlier to smooth the side.

Finally, neaten the top edge with a palette knife. Set the cake aside to dry ready for the next application of icing.

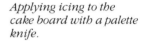

PROFESSIONAL TIP
When cleaning any excess icing from your palette knife after it has been in contact with silver or gold foil of the cake board, always discard this small amount rather than return it to your bowl of icing. This is because the granular texture of the icing and the friction of the knife blade can remove some of the foil. Any traces of silver in the icing will discolour it to a dirty grey.

COATING THE CAKE BOARD

Having completed the coating of the cake you are ready to apply the decoration, unless you decide to coat the cake board first. Many decorators leave the cake board uncoated to expose the silver or gold foil covering, decorating directly on to this with a border, linework or runout pieces. Alternatively, you may like to coat the board with icing to match the top and side coating, or even coat it in a contrasting colour. Coating the board gives a total, finished look to the cake and makes the cake appear larger than it actually is.

To coat the board, place the coated cake on its board on the turntable. Apply the icing to the board using the tip of a palette knife as shown. Using the board edge to scrape the icing off the knife as you rotate the turntable, smooth the icing on to the cake board until it is completely covered. Position the palette knife near the take-off mark on the cake side, holding horizontally to and just above the board. With your other hand, rotate the turntable in one continuous movement until you finish back at the take-off mark. Keeping the knife at the same level, pull it away towards yourself.

To finish the board coating, hold the knife at a slight angle resting on the edge of the cake board as shown. With the other hand, rotate the turntable. This will neaten the edge and create a slight bevel or rounded appearance.

Finally clean the face edge of the cake board with a clean, damp cloth. You can either leave the board face edge exposing the silver or gold, or trim it with ribbon or banding as shown in *Finishing Touches*.

An alternative method for coating the board is to pipe a line of icing using a No. 2 tube (tip) around the edge of the board, then carefully flood-in with runout consistency icing (see page 91) as shown.

Applying icing to the cake board with a palette knife.

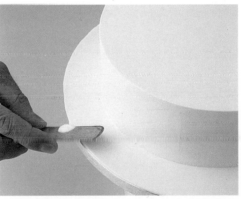

Left: Bevelling the edge of the iced cake board.

Below: Coating the cake board with run-icing.

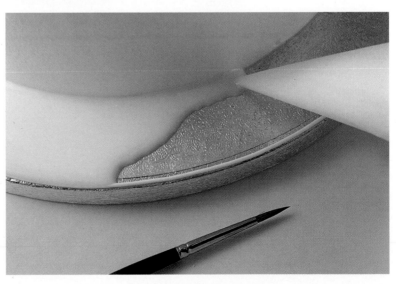

LINEWORK

Delicate linework piping is the basic technique of extruding icing from plain writing tubes (tips) to form straight and curved lines. It is extensively incorporated in the designs of royal iced cakes. The most popular linework is the edging or outlining of shell, bulb and scroll borders, emphasizing the flowing continuity of the design.

Linework is also used on modern cakes which feature runout collars and pre-fabricated off-pieces, again the linework follows the outline of the design to give a total look to the cake, rather than leave edges with an unfinished appearance. Lettering is also a form of linework.

Overpiping is the technique of piping on top of an existing line of piping to make the outline more prominent, or to create a tiered or graduated effect.

LEMON FILIGREE WEDDING CAKE

Delicate in both nature and colour, this spring wedding cake is decorated almost entirely in fine filigree work. The three collar sections feature a primrose motif to match the piped flowers around the base. For the centrepiece, pipe the sections on to waxed paper using freshly made royal icing for added strength.

STARTING LINEWORK PIPING

First of all select the size of tube (tip) you wish to use, examples of which are shown below. When piping linework, take care not to overfill the piping bag with icing. It is more comfortable and easier to pipe using a bag which is only two-thirds full (see *About Royal Icing*).

Linework piping is similar to that of piping borders, both techniques accurately control pressure against speed. The difference between linework piping and border piping is the holding of the bag. With border piping a greater volume of icing with tubes of a wider aperture is used, so the bag is firmly gripped as shown on page 47 in order to force the icing through the tube. With linework piping, which is more delicate, the piping bag is held in a different way.

HOLDING THE PIPING BAG
For best results, hold the bag as shown, using the first finger of the right hand to support the bag underneath, with the thumb of the right hand to keep the bag closed at the top and to apply pressure on the icing to force it through the tube.

Use the first finger of your left hand to steady the bag, simply hold your finger against the bag and use it to stop your other hand shaking during piping – the action of pressing the icing through the bag will inevitably make your hand shake a little, this is when your left hand makes the task much easier with improved results.

(Many teachers show students how to pipe lines using one hand only, this is not good practice and should be avoided.)

STARTING TO PIPE A LINE
Having mastered how to hold the bag, you can now proceed to pipe. Use your thumb to press the icing through the tube, touch the tip of the tube on to the surface to be piped. As soon as you feel the icing attached, start to slowly pull away and a line of icing will be extruded from the tube.

AVOIDING CURLY LINES
If you press too hard, the icing will come out too quickly and the lines will be curly as shown.

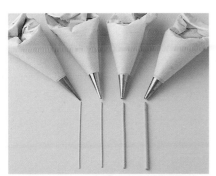
Widths of icing from four writing tubes.

Holding position of the piping bag.

Commencing to pipe a line of icing.

Applying too much pressure.

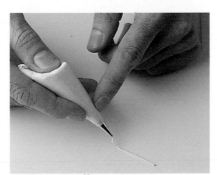
Applying insufficient pressure.

Lifting bag to pipe a curved line.

Avoid starting lines with a bulb.

Avoid ending lines with a bulb.

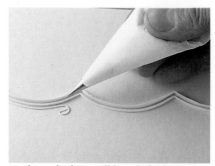

Jerking the bag will break the line.

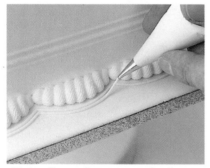

Piping lines adjacent to each other.

Piping in between two parallel lines.

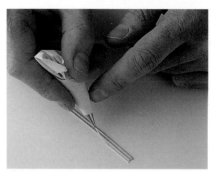

Piping a No. 1 line next to two No. 2s.

AVOIDING BREAKING LINES

If you do not apply sufficient pressure and still move the bag along at the same speed, then the line of icing will most likely break. It is all a matter of regulating the speed with which you pipe to the amount of pressure you apply to the icing.

The same problems arise if you move along too quickly, again the line of icing will break. If you move along too slowly with the same amount of pressure, the lines will be extruded in a curly wavy fashion.

PIPING CURVED LINES

When piping lines, lift the icing well above the surface you are piping on to allow you to control where the line will eventually be dropped. In this way you can pipe straight, curved or wavy lines with the confidence of knowing exactly where they will be positioned. Should you lift the icing too high during piping the line will break – so again a little practice will help you determine the height at which to pipe.

Practice piping curved lines with the aid of a shaped paper template.

AVOIDING BULBS AT THE BEGINNING OF LINES

An important point to watch when piping lines is the start of the line and the finish, avoiding a bulbous shape at each end. The line should be the same width as the tube aperture. Bulbs at the beginning of a line are often caused by not pulling away with the tube once the icing is attached to the surface on which you are piping. As a result the pressure applied forces the icing and forms a bulb because the tube is stationary.

AVOIDING BULBS AT THE END OF LINES

The same problem can occur at the end of a line, again due to not stopping applying pressure when the tube touches the surface a tiny bulb of icing is formed. So to finish a line, lower the line of icing carefully down on to the cake surface. As soon as the tube touches the surface, stop applying pressure, then carefully take the tube away.

AVOIDING UNTIDY END OF LINES

Pulling the tube away with a sudden jerk will cause a pointed untidy end and could lift the line off the surface and distort it.

Having mastered the piping of single lines in straight and curved formations, the linework technique can be used in various ways such as border edging, collar outlining and edging, and lettering.

PIPING ADJACENT LINES

There will no doubt be many occasions when you need to pipe lines adjacent to each other to create a bolder look, to execute a particular style of lettering or to form the basis of tiered linework. Normally as a rule of thumb, the distance between two adjacent lines is equal to the tube (tip) aperture width being used. For example, if a No. 2 tube is used to pipe two adjacent lines, you should be able to comfortably drop a line using the same tube between the two piped lines.

If piping two No. 2 lines, then a No. 1 next to them, the same principle applies. The tube being used to pipe the last line is a No. 1 tube, then the space between the previous line (No. 2) and the present line (No. 1) should be the width of the No. 1 tube aperture.

The side view diagram illustrates two combinations of tiered linework and the tube (tip) sizes used in each build-up.

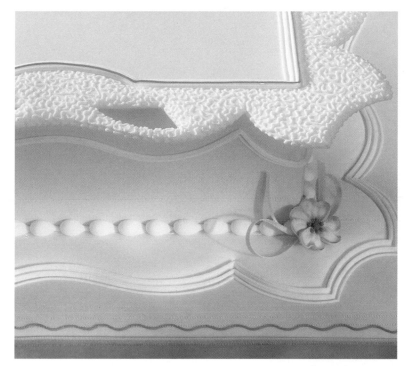

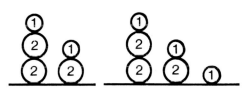

Linework piped in a tiered formation is often used as shown here to integrate top and base runout collars with the overall cake design. A total of six lines is used; building up one, then two and finally three lines high.

OVERPIPING

Overpiping is the technique of piping directly on top of an existing line or border shape to emphasize a shape or to give a tiered or graduated effect. The combination of single adjacent lines described before can be used as it is, or elaborated upon. A popular use of linework piping is the built-up type or tiered linework, used to add interest and give a finished look to border edges, icing coated cake boards and plaques.

Overpiping can be piped immediately on top of icing that has just been piped, or you can allow the icing to dry before overpiping commences. Allowing the icing to dry means that you have a better chance of lifting off a broken line or a mistake, enabling you to re-pipe it. If the icing you are piping on to is still moist, then the overpiped line will bond to it

and make it difficult to remove if necessary.

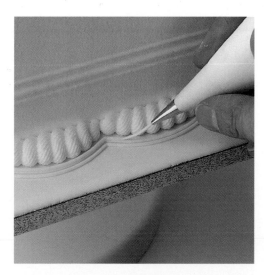

Overpiping a previously piped line.

Linework piped adjacent to a base collar.

Overpiping with a coloured fine line.

When overpiping linework always bear in mind that the highest group of lines should be nearest the edge that you are following, such as a border, collar or plaque. A pleasing combination of tiered linework can be achieved by overpiping the first No. 2 with another No. 2 line followed by a No. 1, making three lines on top of each other. The adjacent series of lines could take the form of a No. 2 line overpiped with a No. 1 line.

To take this example a stage further; if all the lines were piped in base coloured royal icing, it may be appropriate to introduce a contrasting or complementary colour of icing to highlight the work or emphasize the border or collar edge shape being followed. Simply pipe a line of coloured icing using a No. 0 tube (tip) on top of the piped three lines combination – the highest set of lines.

There are numerous combinations of tiered linework, all having their own particular look or application. Overpiped linework is often referred to as 3, 2, 1 linework because of the three lines piped on top of each other, then the two lines piped on top of each other and finally a single line, all piped adjacent to merge or 'blend' a piped border or runout collar with the iced surface of the top or sides of a cake. Experiment with various tube (tip) widths, build up combinations and colour schemes to create the effect you desire.

SCRATCHED LINES

The icing tube (tip) can also be used like a pencil on paper to give a thinner more delicate look than dropped lines. This method involves actually gently resting the piping tube on the iced surface and using it like a pencil to write with the icing. Move the tube along at a constant pressure and speed to pipe wavy, curved and scalloped line designs. Pipe the longest series of shapes that you can

Right: Piping scratched scallop linework.

Far Right: Scratched linework around a cake board.

comfortably pipe, then stop at a join or to make a join. Turn or move the cake slightly and prepare to pipe another section. Attractive scratched line designs are ideal for edging all kinds of borders, runout collars on boards, shaped plaques and for embellishing lettering and numerals.

PIPING LINEWORK ON THE SIDE OF A CAKE

The technique of piping lines on to the side of a cake is exactly the same as piping on the top of a cake, you just need a little more skill to manoeuvre the lines into position, simply because the cake is at an angle. You probably won't need to apply as much pressure and pipe a little slower to give you a chance to accurately position the lines. The use of a template will greatly help, enabling you to repeat a particular design accurately around the cake. For further details on preparing templates, see page 65 and *Templates*.

TILTING THE CAKE
To make the task a little easier support the cake on a block of wood or sturdy object, positioning the cake to the best angle for you to comfortably and neatly pipe. There are many commercially available pieces of apparatus specially designed for working on the sides of cakes, these are normally referred to as cake tilters (see page 9).

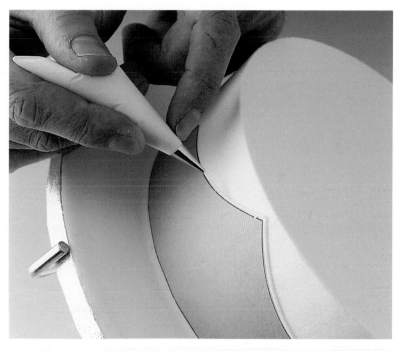

Top Right: When piping on the side of a cake using a cake tilter, the acute angle can make piping difficult. The use of a paper template will ensure accuracy and a consistent repetition of the design.

Right: An attractive cake side design made simpler with the use of a template.

BORDER PIPING

Neatly piped borders of royal icing with attractive flowing designs epitomize the true art of traditional cake decoration. Complemented with overpiping and linework, borders form a frame to adorn the top edge and base of a cake, linking the other aspects of decoration such as the flowers, motif and lettering, in effect holding the design together.

PINK HEART WITH FLOWERS

A delicate tint of pink gives a soft romantic feel to this cake. The bulb border is neatly overpiped, highlighted with a deeper pink colour. Stencilled flowers form the feature decoration with a background of piped leaves. Piped lettering painted silver adds the finishing touch. To ice a heart shaped cake, see page 36.

STARTING BORDER PIPING

Almost all border designs derive from basic tube (tip) aperture shapes, these being the wider plain tubes (No. 3 and 4) and star tubes (No. 5, 6, 7, 8, 42, 43, 44 and 11, 12, 13, 15 and 32). A selection of popular designs is shown overleaf. Plain tubes are used to form basic bulb shapes, plain shells and plain ropes and scrolls. Star tubes make stars, shells, bulbs, ropes, scrolls, rosettes and many more variations. Petal or flower tubes and leaf tubes can also be used to make some interesting alternatives to the more traditional designs.

To pipe bold border work you will need a reasonable amount of icing, more for instance than would be required for linework or tiny edging borders. Make a medium sized piping bag (see page 20) and insert the appropriate tube. Do not overfill the bag, otherwise the icing will seep from the top and make piping difficult and messy. Two-thirds full is a good guide. Fold over the top of the bag before commencing piping.

Hold the bag firmly as shown. For continuous piping of a shell border, the piping bag can be gripped fully in one hand, making piping easier and quicker to complete the border, still take care though holding this way to ensure accuracy and give a neat appearance.

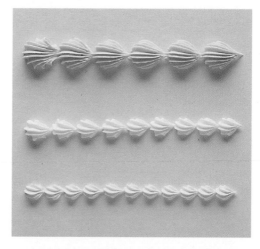

The basic shell border seen here is probably the most widely used design of all. It forms the basis of so many border designs and lends itself beautifully to numerous configurations of overpiping and enhancement with other tubes (tips).

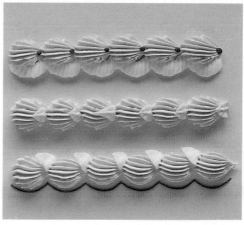

Shells enhanced with leaf tube work (see page 54).

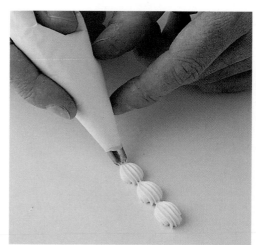

Holding position for border piping.

Continuous piping of a basic shell border.

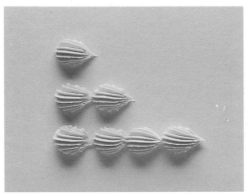

Stages of piping a basic shell border.

SHELLS

Tube (Tip) No. 5, 7, 9, 11, 12, 13 or 15
Position the tube then, without moving the bag, apply pressure using your thumb to extrude icing from the bag. Once the shell has formed a bulbous shape, slowly and gently ease the bag back to form a 'tail'. Position the bag to pipe the next shell so that it just touches the tail of the previous one. Continue to pipe a straight or curved line of shells.

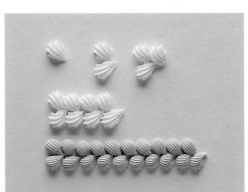

Stages of piping alternating shells.

ALTERNATING SHELLS

Small (No. 5, 7 or 9) or large (No. 11, 12 or 13) star tube (tip)
Use the same technique described for shells but pipe on either side of an imaginary line (use the top edge or base of the cake as the line) from left to right, bringing the tails into the centre at angle of about 45 degrees. Start with the second shell slightly lower than the first as a guide, then continue piping so that each shell piped just touches the previous one.

Stages of piping a fleur-de-lis.

FLEUR-DE-LIS

Small medium or large star or rope tube (tip) No. 5, 7, 9, 11, 12, 13 or 15, depending on the size of decoration required
First pipe a central elongated shell with a long tail. Next pipe a curved shell on the left, bringing the tail to a point and finish at the same point as the centre shell. To complete the fleur-de-lis, pipe a curved shell from the right, again finish with a pointed tail at the same place as the two previously piped shells.

Piping stars using various tube (tip) sizes.

STARS

Tube (Tip) No. 5, 7, 9, 11, 12, 13 or 15
Pipe stars using small or large star tubes, depending upon the size of cake they are to decorate. Hold the bag upright, force the icing out to the size of star required and then pull up to form a point.

Providing the size and shape is consistent, stars make a very easy-to-pipe border design or can be used to cover large areas on the top or sides of cakes. Try piping stars on to waxed paper, then when dry attach to the cake.

ROSETTES
Tube (Tip) No. 42, 43 or 44
The tubes selected for rosette piping should usually have finer indentations than those of star tubes.

Again with the bag held almost upright to the surface on which you are piping, force out the icing and move the bag in a circular motion, lifting the bag slightly as you pipe. To finish a rosette, bring the tube into the centre and pull off gently to form a neat tail.

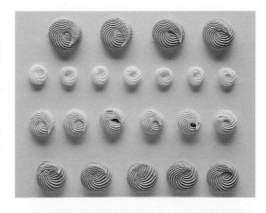

Piping rosettes in varying sizes.

TWISTED ROPE
Plain writing tube (tip) No. 2, 3 or 4, rope tube (tip) No. 42, 43, 44 or star tube (tip) No. 5, 7, 9, 11, 12, 13 or 15, depending on the effect required
Hold the bag in the conventional manner, position the tube, then press to extrude the icing. Keeping a constant pressure and speed (to keep a consistent width), twist the bag as you pipe in a clockwise or anti-clockwise circular motion.

Twisted rope borders using various tubes (tips).

SCROLLS
Rope tube (tip) No. 11, 12, 13, 15 or 44
To pipe 'S' and 'C' scrolls on to a cake it is preferable to have a chamfered top edge, so that the scrolls sit at an angle and look comfortable on the cake. The scrolls should be piped positioned half on the top of the cake and half on the side.

A suitable chamfered edge can be produced at the end of the final coating stage. Simply hold the knife at an angle of about 45 degrees to the edge and rotate the turntable to remove the icing and create the chamfered edge. Alternatively, use a small sharp knife to shave the dry icing off while rotating the turntable.

Piping 'S' scrolls and 'C' scrolls.

'S' Scrolls
Position the tube, then use the same technique as the rosette to start with. Instead of taking the tube into the centre, come out of the flow and work in an opposite curve. Gradually reduce the pressure and form a neatly graduated pointed tail.

'C' Scrolls
Using a similar technique to the 'S' scroll, but work in an anti-clockwise motion and form a large sweeping curve with a graduated pointed tail.

Combined 'S' and 'C' Scrolls
Having mastered the individual techniques of piping scrolls, you can design numerous combinations from the two basic shapes, by piping them in twos and threes and facing them in different directions. Also if you twist the tube as you pipe (see Twisted Rope) an attractive rope scroll can be formed.

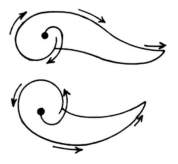

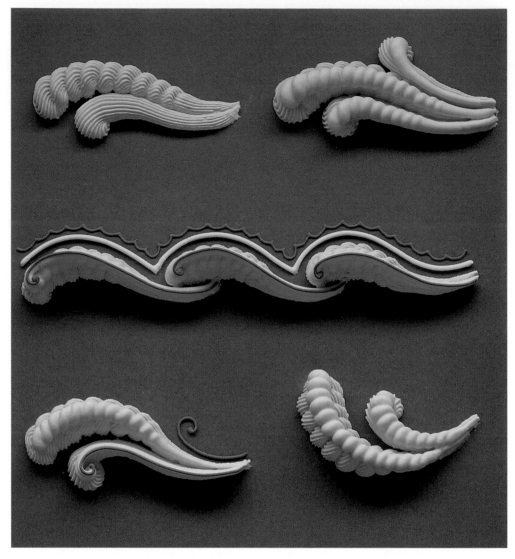

The basic 'S' and 'C' scroll shapes are particularly suited to combining together. The smooth flowing shapes follow similar curves in places, it is here that the two shapes connect beautifully. Further decoration can be added to the combinations by the introduction of overpiping as shown.

RAISED TRELLIS
Tube (Tip) No. 42, 43 or 44 and tube (tip) No. 2 and 1

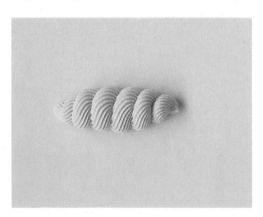

1 First stage in piping raised trellis.

This is a traditional style of decorative piping. It is a good piping exercise and, even though it is quite time consuming, a form of decoration that will no doubt find its place on your cakes.

The whole decoration can be built up completely with trellis, but you will find it quicker and still as attractive to first pipe an oval shaped scroll using a fine rope tube.

Step 1
To make the oval scroll, position the rope tube and apply pressure to the bag to extrude the icing. Pipe in a rope fashion, starting off narrow, then wider in the middle and finally narrow at the end to match the shape of the opposite end.

Step 2

Start to pipe the trellis on to the oval base. Use a No. 2 tube to pipe parallel diagonal lines as shown. Overpipe again in the opposite direction.

Step 3

Continue to build up the trellis using a finer tube as you reach the last few sets of lines. Remember to pipe the net in different directions for each layer.

BULBS

Tube (Tip) No. 3 or 4

Piping bulbs involves holding the piping bag in a slightly different way to shell piping. Two-thirds fill a bag with very slightly softened icing (add a few drops of cold water) – not runny but firm enough to retain its shape when piped. Position the tube, holding the bag almost upright as shown. Keep the tube just slightly away from the cake surface and apply pressure to the bag to extrude the icing. Keeping the tube in and just below the surface of the bulb, continue piping steadily lifting the tube slightly all the time until the desired bulb shape is formed. To remove the tube, lift it level to the surface of the bulb and using a quick but fairly accurate sideways movement 'cut' the icing level. Use a slightly moistened fine paint brush to 'blend' the cut-off mark into the bulb and make a perfect surface.

If, when the bulbs have been piped, they 'sag' a little and start to merge into each other, either the icing is too soft or the bulbs are being piped too close together. If you intend to overpipe the bulbs, allow them to crust over just a little prior to overpiping as any movement on the semi-soft icing could start them flowing and merging into each other. To set the bulbs quickly and thus prevent any distortion of shape, place them beneath the gentle warmth of a reading lamp with a flexible arm for a few minutes to set the outer surface of the icing. An alternative method of applying bulbs to a cake is to pipe them on to waxed paper and allow to dry, then position and attach them to the cake with royal icing.

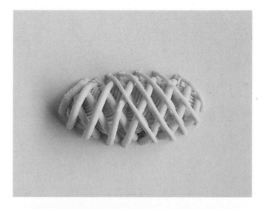

2 Overpiping the basic trellis pattern.

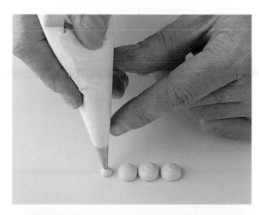

3 The completed raised trellis section.

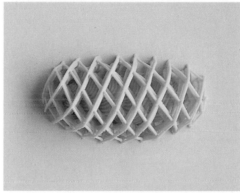

Holding position of bag for piping bulbs.

If necessary use a lightly moistened fine paint brush to flatten and remove the points on the bulbs before they dry completely. If you are very careful you can do the same using the moistened tip of your little finger.

DOTS, BEADS AND PEARLS
Tube (Tip) No. 000, 00, 0, 1 or 2
Use exactly the same method as for bulb piping, but smaller tubes in smaller piping bags are used with less pressure being applied.

Many interesting and attractive configurations of dots, beads and pearls can be integrated into every aspect of cake decoration. A few examples are shown here to give ideas from which you can develop your own designs.

Neatly executed bulb borders add an elegant quite formal look to a cake, especially when overpiped with fine lines and a touch of coloured icing. Once the line or curve of bulbs is piped, there are numerous combinations of linework, dots, beads and pearls that can be used to enhance the basic shapes.

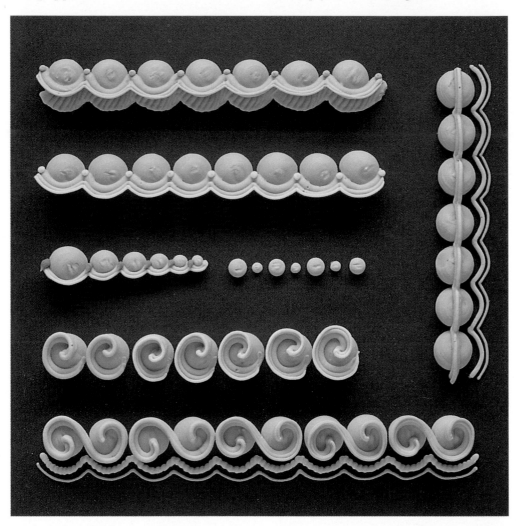

OVERPIPING BORDERS
Tube (Tip) No. 0, 1, 2 and wider plain tube No. 3 and 4
All piped borders can be further enhanced by the use of overpiping. Endless permutations of widths in ropes and plain, along with various colour combinations, can make an ordinary border into a more interesting aspect of the cake design.

It is normal practice for overpiping to follow the shape of the basic border or individual shell or bulb. Overpiping can commence immediately after the piping of the border is complete; there is no need to allow the icing to dry or crust. Use icing of a good piping consistency, not too stiff, this will assist in the formation of neatly flowing curves. Continue to build up with lines using finer tubes until the desired effect or amount of overpiping is achieved.

Also 'C' scrolls and 'S' scrolls can greatly benefit from overpiping.

A selection of piped borders using star and rope tubes (tips). The shape of the basic shell, star, barrel or rope lends itself to overpiping which follows and emphasizes the shape. The use of a darker colour of icing for fine overpiping further enhances the attractively flowing shapes.

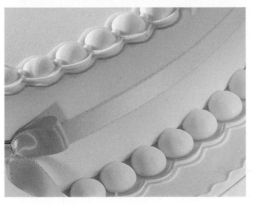

Far Left: Basic bulb border with overpiping.

Left: Basic shell border with overpiping.

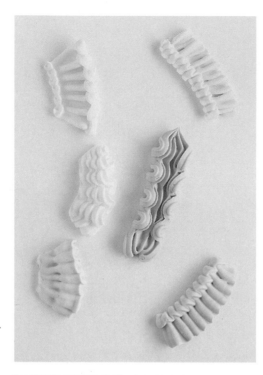

Using frilling tubes (tips), various attractive patterns can be created each with its own suitability to a particular application or cake design.

Cutting a leaf tube piping bag.

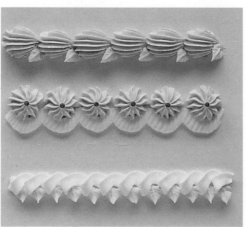

FRILLING TUBES

Cakes covered in sugarpaste and decorated with a Garrett frill have caught the eye of many royal icing enthusiasts; so much so that a series of frilling tubes (tips) has been developed in order to emulate the frill decoration in royal icing. There are various configurations available, each giving a different effect and each with their own individual style.

The procedure for filling the bag is the same as that described for border piping. A medium to large bag will be required so that continuous piping can be carried out, to create long lengths of decoration with the minimum number of joins. Use fresh royal icing that is well beaten to full peak stage (see page 15) so that when piped it will retain the detail of the frill effect. With the open slot of the tube facing upward, pipe frills on to the cake. A regular outward and side-to-side movement will create an attractive decoration. Varying the movements will allow you to create your own unique designs using this exciting new piping tube.

PETAL AND LEAF TUBE (TIP) BORDERS

Tube (Tip) No. 57, 58 or 59

Unusually interesting effects can be achieved using petal and leaf tubes to create border designs. They can be used on their own or in conjunction with shell, scroll and bulb borders. Try also incorporating some linework into the design as shown.

The diagram shows cutting a leaf tube from a conventional paper piping bag (see also page 80).

Above Left: Frilling tubes (tips) are now widely available in a range of designs and provide the royal icing enthusiast with a tool to emulate a similar effect to that of the Garrett frill normally associated with sugarpaste covered cakes.

Left: Borders with leaf tube embellishments.

BLUE TEDDY BEAR CAKE

A traditional piped shell design with overpiping forms the attractive edging to this child's cake. On the cake board, simple linework, a scratched line and a trimming of blue velvet complete the decoration. The blue teddy is directly painted on to a round runout plaque as described in Painting. See also Templates for the teddy bear.

CAKE DESIGN

As with all aspects of cake decoration, good preparation is also essential when planning to make and decorate a cake. Good design is the key to an attractive cake that is pleasing to the eye; it should appeal to everyone before it is even cut into slices for eating.

The design of the cake really starts before the fruit cake is even mixed and baked.

A selection of the wide variety of specially shaped cake tins now available.

SHAPE

The first decision to be made by you or the customer is the shape of cake. With the wide variety of specially shaped cake tins now available, choosing one can be quite difficult.

The best plan is to first sketch out a few rough drawings of ideas you have in mind. Cakes that have caught your eye in books or at shows and exhibitions may have interested you so much that you wish to make one yourself. Do not be over-ambitious, select something that you can manage to decorate successfully to your present ability. Never be tempted to copy a really advanced design that you know will probably result in unsatisfactory results – especially if you intend to charge for it!

SIZE

The size of the cake is usually governed by two factors – the number of portions required or the actual cost of the finished cake! The following chart is a guide to help you decide on the size of cake tin to use.

PORTIONS

The calculations listed are based on portions of 2.5 cm (1 inch) squares. Remember it is always a good idea to over-estimate the number of portions required rather than have insufficient on the day!

Square	Portions	Round	Portions
13 cm (5 inch)	16	13 cm (5 inch)	14
15 cm (6 inch)	27	15 cm (6 inch)	22
18 cm (7 inch)	40	18 cm (7 inch)	30
20 cm (8 inch)	54	20 cm (8 inch)	40
23 cm (9 inch)	70	23 cm (9 inch)	54
25 cm (10 inch)	90	25 cm (10 inch)	68
27.5 cm (11 inch)	112	27.5 cm (11 inch)	86
30 cm (12 inch)	134	30 cm (12 inch)	100

Note Shaped cakes, such as heart, hexagonal, octagonal and petal, will give approximately the same number of portions as a round cake of the same size.

WEDDING CAKE PORTIONS

	Portions Square Cake	Portions Round Cake
2 Tier – 18 and 25 cm (7 and 10 inch)	130	98
3 Tier – 13, 18, 23 cm (5, 7, 9 inch)	126	98
3 Tier – 15, 20, 25 cm (6, 8, 10 inch)	171	130

Remember if you only require a particular size of cake for the actual celebration table, but find that more portions of cake will be required, you can always make a cutting cake. This is a separate cake that is just marzipanned and flat coated without any decoration. Extra portions can then be cut from this cake and served or given to those not attending the celebration.

THE PLAN

At this stage you will be taking into account all factors, such as colour, decoration, lettering etc. The best idea is to make a drawing of the cake top (plan) and side (side elevation) on a large sheet of paper.

For a good representation of what the cake will look like, use coloured pencils to lightly colour the background, this depicts the base colour. The decoration and lettering can also be drawn on and coloured, even down to the ribbon used to edge the cake board. If you cannot draw too well, make tracings of each item and move them around on the cake plan until a pleasing balance is achieved.

Keep the cake plan as a reference as you ice and decorate the cake at each stage.

Drawing a cake plan and side elevation.

Tracing a border design on to the plan.

PROFESSIONAL TIP
Further detailed reading and diagrams on cake design can be found in the book Confectionery Design, published by Merehurst Limited.

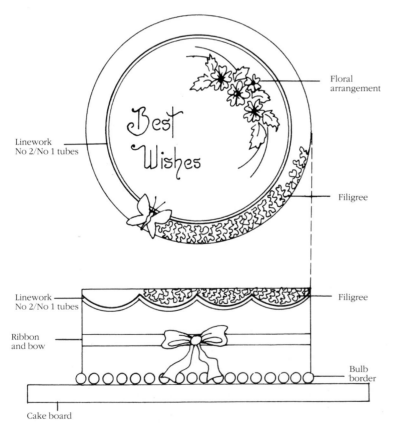

Floral arrangement

Linework
No 2/No 1 tubes

Filigree

Linework
No 2/No 1 tubes

Filigree

Ribbon
and bow

Bulb
border

Cake board

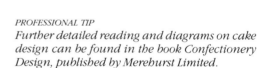

The completed cake plan and side elevation with all the necessary design and practical specification included ready to execute as a 'real' cake.

BASE COLOUR

Choose a suitable colour scheme to enhance the theme of the cake. This needs to suit the recipient of the cake whether it be a child, teenager or older person. The choice of colour should reflect their age group and personality; although this is not always true and some people may prefer quite the reverse in design and colour. A child's cake will probably have bright, lively colours, whereas a cake for an older person would look nicer in a soft subtle pastel tint. If in doubt, use a neutral colour such as biscuit, see page 19.

COLOUR SCHEMES

Having selected your overall base colour, you then need to introduce other colours that will greatly enhance the overall appearance. Use these colours as part of your feature decoration or to emphasize borders, linework or to pipe the name or inscription.

There are three main types of colour scheme to use in cake decoration – monochromatic, complementary, harmonious – unless you choose the very modern and futuristic designs which let your imagination run riot, such as the triangular Blue Jazz cake on page 82.

White is a good base if you are new to using colour. This safe way of introducing yourself to colour schemes means that you can experiment with colour on white before trying out some of the more involved schemes detailed here.

THE COLOUR SPECTRUM
Before introducing other colours you should really have a basic knowledge of the colour spectrum and the way in which colours work with each other.

The colour spectrum consists of three primary colours; red, blue and yellow. By mixing equal quantities of any two of these colours, a further or secondary colour will be produced – red and yellow make orange, blue and yellow make green and blue and red make violet. Similar effects will be achieved if food colours are combined in the same way. The colour spectrum therefore provides an invaluable source of reference for all colour sugarcraft work. It can also be seen that the spectrum has light values from light to dark, for instance yellow has the lightest value through to violet which has the darkest value. These basic principles provide us with the necessary information to start creating colour schemes for cakes.

By mixing and blending this wide range of colours together, an infinite range of shades is obtained. Even colours like dark blue and black can really add an extra dimension to the work of the cake decorator.

The Cake Designer's Colour Spectrum
This chart illustrates quite simply the basic primary, secondary and tertiary colours along with the colour values of light (yellow) to dark (violet). The chart can also be used to define the basic colour schemes – monochromatic, complementary and harmonious.

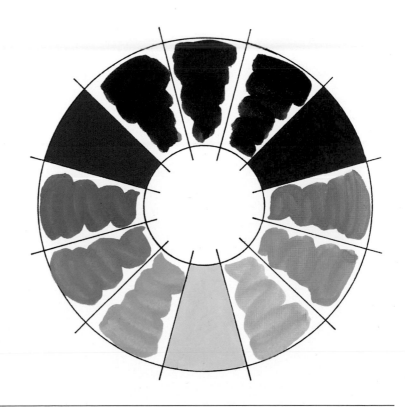

MONOCHROMATIC

The easiest colour scheme of all to work with is when only one colour is employed. Start by coating the cake in a pale tint of the colour, a slightly stronger colour for the piping, scrolls, shells and so on, then an even stronger colour for the fine piping of linework and inscription.

COMPLEMENTARY

This method makes use of contrasting or complementary colours. Colours which are opposite each other on the spectrum are used together, for example yellow and violet make an attractive twosome. The rule to remember is to use the colours in a scheme from light to dark. If you look at the base of the spectrum, yellow is the lightest and violet is the darkest. Do not use a violet background with a yellow flower on, even equal amounts of two opposite colours can look garish!

HARMONIOUS

The most complicated scheme to work with is colour harmony. This is achieved when three to six adjacent colours on the spectrum are used together. Most of the colour should be in a pale pastel tint, not too pale however as it will look washed out or dirty. Then introduce a few darker tints and shades.

NEUTRAL COLOURS

Colours such as biscuit, cream, coffee and chocolate can also be used to good effect. You will find that most colours can be added to these neutral bases from pale tints to red, blue, orange, green, brown and black.

FEATURE DECORATION

When you first decide to or are asked to make the cake, try to find out the interests, hobby or pastime of the recipient. Having an idea of the theme of the cake will help you decide in what form to make the feature decoration. It could be a spray of flowers, a runout plaque of a particular shape, painted to depict a favourite hobby or pastime, or a piped figure or animal motif. Or you may be given a badge or company logo to copy for a special celebration cake for a club or organization. If the person the cake is intended for has several interests to depict or belongs to different clubs and organisations, you will need a multi sided cake, such as a hexagonal or octagonal shape. Simple examples are placing a square plaque on a square cake or an oval spray of flowers on an oval cake as shown.

All this information will inspire you and help you make a decision about the shape of the cake required to carry the decoration.

INSCRIPTION

If the cake requires an inscription, greeting or name to be piped on, take this into consideration when planning the feature decoration for the cake top. Do not under any circumstances overcrowd the cake with too much decoration, it will look fussy and untidy. Read the information in *Lettering* regarding choosing a suitable style and colour of lettering to complement the theme and the tastes of the recipient of the cake.

OVERALL BALANCE

After making decisions about base colour, piped borders or runout collars, feature decoration and inscription, take a look at the plan and check over it for any final details you may have forgotten, such as ribbon trimmings and edging for the board. Then stand back and ask yourself does the cake look pleasingly balanced? Is the decoration spaced to give an airy open feel and not a cluttered look? Is the decoration evenly spaced to create an overall balance and not confined to one side or all at the top? If you can confidently say yes to all these questions, then you are ready to go ahead with the design; if not make adjustments or ask a friend for their view, until you are quite happy with the result.

RUGBY CLUB CAKE

This multi-sided cake lends itself ideally to the subject, as the hexagon provides six panels in which to depict various sporting positions. The club badge is painted on to a runout plaque and the rugby balls made in a similar manner. For the trophies, simply pipe a series of bulbs, allow them to dry and then attach them together with royal icing. The cup part is made similar to the bells described in Pressure Piping, scoop out the centre and allow to dry. Attach the cup to the stem along with two piped handles. Paint the trophy with silver food colour and paint the base black.

REDUCTION AND ENLARGEMENT OF DESIGNS

There will be several occasions when you find a template or pattern for a cake decoration that is either too large or too small to fit the allocated space. Given below are a few suggestions to help you overcome this problem.

PHOTOCOPYING MACHINE

The easiest answer would be to take the drawing to your local print shop and ask for the image to be reduced or enlarged on their photocopying machine.

PANTOGRAPH

This fairly inexpensive implement is made from plastic or metal and available from good art and craft shops. A pointer follows the outline of the original drawing, while a pencil on the other end of the pantograph transfers the reduced or enlarged image. If your design alteration is just a one-off, a pantograph is not really worthwhile.

GRID COPYING

For the majority of people the most readily available method is the grid system. This is a reasonably simple way of changing the size and still keeping it in proportion. Draw a grid of squares over the design to be altered, an average size of greeting card can be divided into 2 cm (¾ inch) squares. Then draw a second grid on another sheet of paper with larger or smaller squares, calculating these as closely as possible to fractions of the squares in the original grid.

Number and letter the squares on both the grids identically for easy cross-reference during the copying process. Follow the outlines from the original and copy them carefully on to the prepared grid. Using the squares as guidelines,

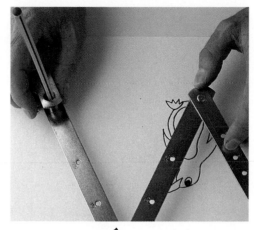

Enlarging a drawing using a pantograph.

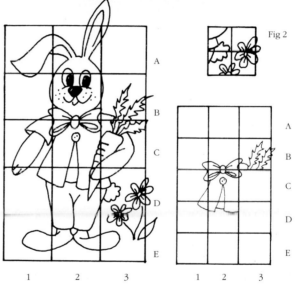

copy for example the carrot top and the tip of the rabbit's shoulder from the B3 square and so on until the picture is complete. You can sub-divide any square to give you more guidelines which are useful for intricate sections such as the D3 square as shown in Fig. 2.

COPYRIGHT INFRINGEMENT

Please note that references in this book recommending that you adapt designs from greeting cards, gift wrapping paper and books is for your own personal cake decorating as a hobby. If you intend to use these designs on cakes that are made to order for sale or offered for sale, you must first obtain permission from the rightful copyright owner of the design. Using the designs without the correct permission is a serious infringement of copyright.

TRANSFERRING DESIGNS ON TO CAKES

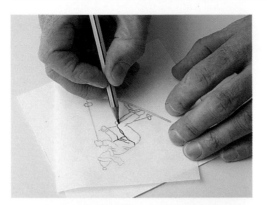

Outlining a design on to tracing paper.

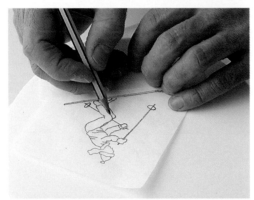

Transferring the image on to the icing.

Using a scriber to prick the design on to the icing.

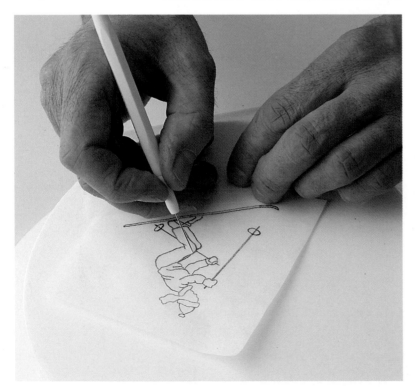

TRACING ON TO PAPER

To transfer a design on to a cake from a book or your own design, you will first need to trace the image from the page. Using tracing paper or greaseproof (waxed) paper, place it over the design and outline carefully and neatly with an HB pencil. Use one of the following methods to transfer the design on to the cake:

TRACING ON TO ICING

Turn the tracing over and outline the design using a slightly harder pencil such as a 2H; using a soft pencil may result in smudge marks on the icing surface. Place the tracing in position on the cake and transfer the design by following the outline using a 2H pencil.

PIN-PRICKING

Trace the design from the paper as before. Instead of reversing the tracing to outline it, place the tracing on to the iced surface. Secure the tracing temporarily with masking tape, if required. Follow the outline using a sugarcraft scriber, mapping pen or similar implement to transfer a dotted image on to the icing. Make the dots as close or distant as required to make a recognizable outline. However, do not press into the icing too much as this could damage it.

MAKING A CAKE SIDE TEMPLATE

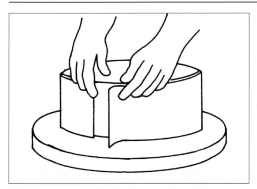

Measuring the paper to fit the cake side.

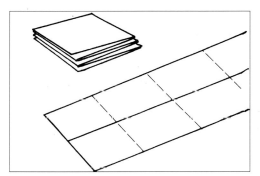

Dividing into desired number of sections.

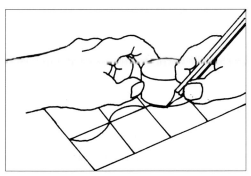

Transferring on the required design.

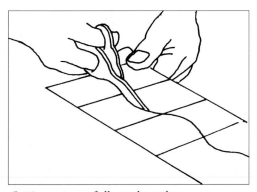

Cutting out carefully and neatly.

There will be several occasions in cake decorating when you need to make a template for the side of the cake, simply refer back to this section for the instructions.

Cut a length of cartridge paper to fit around the coated cake. The paper strip should be the height of the cake side. With the paper strip flat, draw an accurately measured line down the centre of the length of the paper.

Measure the length of the paper and divide into the number of sections required. Mark the measured sections on each side of the paper, then draw a line across.

In each measured section draw in the required shape; to produce a wavy line for this template, use a suitably sized round object, such as a pastry cutter. Alternate the curves as shown to create a continuous wavy line.

Cut neatly along the wavy line to produce two template shapes. Only one is needed.

Replace the template around the cake and secure with a small piece of masking tape. Start and finish piping or decorating at the take-off mark and eventually make this the back of the cake so that any joins will not be visible.

PROFESSIONAL TIP
Any templates that you intend to use frequently can be copied on to paper, then pasted on to thin card and covered with self adhesive clear plastic film; this will enable you to attach waxed paper with masking tape for runout work or pressure piping. When finished, it can be wiped clean ready for the next time.

A template was used for this cake side decoration.

TEXTURES AND EFFECTS

There are various textures and effects that can be created by using the basic techniques of piping, linework and coating, including basic, tube and brush embroidery, basket weave and various cake side effects. All these techniques can be incorporated into most cake designs to add further interest.

BASIC EMBROIDERY

Right: Using small aperture writing tubes (tips), an infinite variety of line designs and floral images can be created from very basic dots, pulled dots, lines and curves.

Below: This attractive runout plaque is decorated with a lily of the valley design, using pressure piping for the flowers and tube embroidery for the leaves.

Piped embroidery on cakes has been used for many years and very fine examples can be seen in many of the 'collector' cake decoration books by famous authors. Basic embroidery is simply a combination of curved lines, straight lines, dots, bulbs, leaf and petal shapes tastefully arranged to produce an attractive, delicate design. Embroidery can be piped on the top or side of the cake or on prepared plaques which can then be attached to the cake after decorating. If you intend to pipe embroidery on to the side of a cake, first tilt the cake, see cake tilters on page 9.

These edible place settings make an unusual feature for a special celebration, such as an anniversary, children's party or wedding reception. Make the base from two runout oblong shapes joined together at an angle with royal icing. Pipe on the embroidery design and the name of the guest using coloured icing.

An edible runout table place setting.

BRODERIE ANGLAISE

Prepare the basic background as a runout, leaving holes to form the flower and any border design. When dry, pipe the detail around the holes using fine piping tubes (tips) and coloured icing.

A delicately beautiful runout plaque that could be used as a centrepiece for an engagement cake. The plaque is decorated with a broderie anglaise finish and features pressure piped love birds (see page 102) and stencilled pink hearts. See Templates for the design.

TUBE (TIP) EMBROIDERY

As with many other aspects of modern cake decoration, embroidery has undergone a well deserved revival and many cake decorators are discovering the fascinating art of tube (tip) embroidery.

Tube embroidery as the name implies is performed using a tube to reproduce embroidery stitches used in needlework. The technique is based on linework piping and scratched lines (see page 44) – remember the principles of pressure and movement control as you pipe. There are many basic stitches you first need to practice.

Opposite: The finished plaque with brush embroidered flower and foliage (described overleaf) looks particularly pleasing on a similar coloured background with writing of a deeper tint.

Right: All tube embroidery designs are based on one or more of the basic stitches illustrated here. Use fine writing tubes (tips), such as No. 00, 0 and 1, to create a realistic reproduction of cotton and silk embroidery.

RUNNING STITCH
Pipe short lines of the same size with a space between.

BACK STITCH
Pipe as for running stitch leaving smaller spaces in between.

STEM STITCH
Pipe short lines in a line, each should slightly overlap the previous one.

HERRINGBONE
Pipe a diagonal line from top left to bottom right. The next line is piped in the opposite direction and crosses the previous stitch at its base, the third line repeats the first and so on.

CROSS-STITCH
Simply pipe a cross of two lines of equal length that overlap in the centre.

FISHBONE STITCH
First pipe a central vein, then pipe an angled line from the outside to cross over the vein. The second stitch is piped from the opposite direction and again crosses over the vein. Useful for piping leaves.

CHAIN STITCH
Pipe a leaf shape, then pipe a second leaf starting inside the open end of the first.

LAZY DAISY
Pipe a circle of shapes each with a small line piped over the rounded ends.

FEATHER STITCH
Pipe small U shaped curves in opposite directions as shown, which start just above the centre of the previous stitch.

BUTTONHOLE
Pipe a right angle corner shape as shown, across and then down. The second stitch starts inside the corner of the first.

BUTTON WHEEL
Pipe as for the buttonhole but make the lines radiate to a centre to form a circle.

SEED STITCH
Very simple, just pipe a series of dots quite closely together; makes an ideal centre for flowers.

LONG AND SHORT STITCH

Pipe alternating long lines and short lines in a row. Pipe the second and subsequent rows to fill in the gaps of the previous row.

FRENCH KNOTS

Pipe a small circle and continue piping to fill in the centre. Pull the tube away to resemble the tail of a knot.

Having practised the basic stitches you can then employ the techniques in various ways to produce plaques, cake top features and decorative designs to embellish runout work.

TUBE (TIP) EMBROIDERED PLAQUES

The patterns for the plaques in the photographs can be found in *Templates*, but you could quite easily adapt a favourite design from a needlework or embroidery book.

To decorate a plaque with embroidery, first trace the design (see *Cake Design*, page 64) on to a prepared runout plaque. Make up several piping bags with fine tubes (tips) such as No. 1, 0 and 00, each filled with different coloured icing. Pipe the design using the basic embroidery stitches.

Right: Some examples of tube embroidery in designs that can easily be adapted to suit various themes. The careful planning of colours and the correct choice of stitch are essential to producing appealing work.

BRUSH EMBROIDERY

This method of decoration in royal icing produces stunning effects. Once the basic technique is perfected, you can spend many enjoyable hours creating your own designs and special effects.

A selection of designs (including the ones shown here) suitable for brush embroidery can be found in *Templates* or you may like to create your own by adapting pictures from books.

Prepare a cupful of royal icing and add about 5 ml (1 tsp) of clear piping gel. This will soften the icing slightly and give it a smoother surface. More importantly it will retard the drying time, giving you longer to brush and work the icing. After some practise you may find that you can work the icing quickly enough without adding piping gel.

Prepare a small piping bag with a No. 1 tube (tip) and two-thirds fill with prepared icing.

PROFESSIONAL TIP
For brush embroidery, use quality sable brushes with a good spring to the bristles. Hair type brushes are unsuitable for this type of work.

Step 1
Transfer your design to the iced surface of the cake or plaque, using one of the methods on page 64. Always start with the part of the design which appears to be furthest away from you. This will give added depth and interest to the finished work. Working on a small area at a time, pipe an outline of one petal of a flower as shown.

Step 2
Flood just inside the line using various pressure on the bag to create thicker and thinner widths as shown. With a small, moist paintbrush, brush the icing down towards the centre of the flower.

Step 3
Continue using the same technique until you complete the flower, finishing with the petal nearest to you.

1 Pipe and outline shape of first petal.

2 Brush the icing to the flower centre.

3 Complete all petals.

4 Pipe stem on and outline leaf.

5 Complete both leaves.

6 Pipe on leaf vein and flower stamens.

With practice and a little care, you will probably find that you do not need to outline the shapes each time. Simply use the soft icing to form a neat outline and then follow the brush-working technique.

Step 4

Pipe on the stem and outline the leaf. To create a bolder line, outline twice, once on the actual design outline and then slightly inside but parallel to the first line.

Step 5

Complete both leaves. Leave the brush embroidery to dry.

Step 6

When all the brush work is complete and dry, pipe in the detail such as stamen in the flower centres and veins in the leaves. Use tube (tip) No. 0 or No. 00 with suitably coloured icing for these finishing touches.

Basket weave in royal icing is used extensively to produce attractive 'containers' to fill with flowers and ribbons. This tiny cake would make an ideal centrepiece decoration for a cake or can be used as a small gift or even a table place setting.

BASKET WEAVE

Flowers are used extensively in cake decoration so there is frequently the need for a container to display them in. Baskets of flowers are always popular, either used as a theme for the full cake, or as small decorations for the tops and sides of cakes.

To pipe basket weave, you will need a No. 22 tube (tip) or for smaller work use a plain tube, such as a No. 3. You will also need a plain tube No. 2 or 3 (depending upon the size of the basket tube being used). If you want to create the basket weave effect using smaller tubes, you can make your own by carefully flattening a small rope tube such as a No. 44, using pliers.

Prepare piping bags with the basket colour of your choice. You may like to use one colour for the plain tube and another colour icing for the actual basket weave.

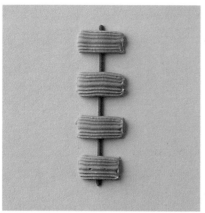 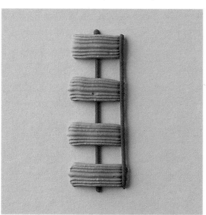 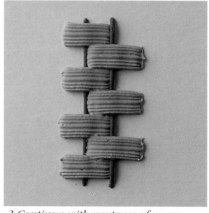

1 Start the weave over the vertical line.   *2 Repeat with another vertical line.*   *3 Continue with next row of weave.*

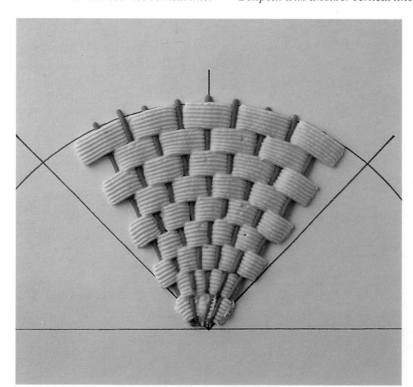

Step 1
Using the plain tube (tip), pipe a vertical line. With the basket weave tube, pipe short horizontal bands as shown. The distance between each band should be the width of the basket weave tube. Ensure that the bands are all the same length.

Step 2
Pipe a second vertical line with the plain tube just resting on the right hand edges of the bands.

Step 3
Again pipe short horizontal bands, this time in between the first piped ones. Repeat the technique to complete the basket weave.

Left: For shaped baskets you will need to radiate the straight lines out from the narrowest point. The bands of basket weave will also need to be increased or decreased in width to fit the shape.

CAKE SIDE EFFECTS

As well as the basic coating techniques described in *Coating Techniques*, there are various other ways in which the side of a cake can be made more interesting and unusual.

Once you have gained experience in the handling of icing and how to coat a cake successfully, you will understand the characteristics of royal icing, enabling you to exploit its potential. Here are a few ideas to give you some inspiration. (See page 37 for more effects.)

TWO-COLOUR COMB SCRAPER
Coat the side of the cake in the conventional manner using a darker colour than the top. When dry, apply the final coating of icing using the same colour as the cake top. Use a comb scraper with the points of the teeth trimmed off.

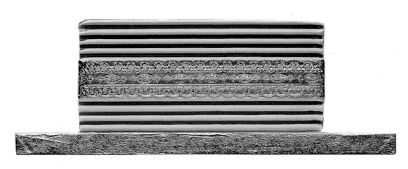

SUGAR TEXTURED BORDER
Coat the cake in the conventional manner and allow to dry completely. Cut two bands of strong cartridge paper to fit around the cake as masking templates. Attach the masks to create a space between, secure the bands with masking tape. Apply icing to the side of the cake using a palette knife and take the cake side scraper around as if making a final coat. Tilt the cake and carefully throw coloured (see page 81) caster (superfine) or granulated sugar at the moist band of icing. Remove the masking templates and allow the icing to dry before adding any further decoration. The sugar textured technique can also be used to make decorations such as a butterfly.

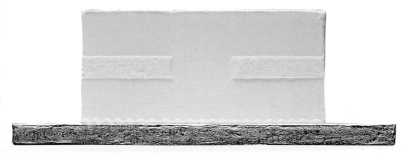

SMOCKING
A realistic reproduction of smocking can be achieved by using a comb scraper in a vertical rather than horizontal position on the final coat of the cake side (square cakes only). While the icing is still soft, pinch at intervals as shown using plastic tweezers dipped into water. Allow the icing to dry, then using a No. 1 tube (tip) pipe on the needlework stitches with icing of a suitable colour.

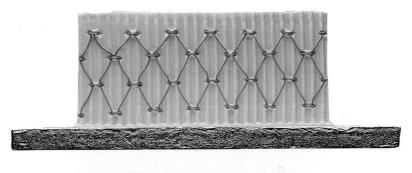

STIPPLED ICING BORDER
Using the same basic preparation as Sugar Textured Border, make a template of your choice. Attach to the cake and apply icing using a palette knife, this time stipple the icing using a piece of foam sponge. Remove the template.

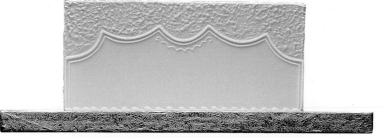

FLOWER PIPING

Above: A simple but attractive arrangement of flowers piped using the pulled method described here.

Flowers and cake decoration go hand-in-hand. As a form of decoration, flowers have always been used extensively and very often form the main feature or focal point of a decorated cake. Royal iced flowers can be made using various techniques, such as stencilling (see page 113), brush embroidery, tube embroidery (see *Textures and Effects*) and of course the traditional piped flowers made using a flower nail.

Here are the techniques for making piped royal iced flowers with or without flower nails, with examples of how to attractively arrange and position the flowers on cakes.

PIPED FLOWERS WITHOUT A FLOWER NAIL

Simple yet attractive piped flowers can be made from royal icing using a piping technique without a flower nail.

This method of piping flowers relies on two basic petal shapes, using small plain tubes (tips) No. 1 or 2, a bulb pulled out to a spike to form a pointed petal and a bulb with the spike or point facing into the centre of the flower. The technique involves piping the basic petal shape into formations of the number of petals you require. A more natural effect can be achieved by making the petals less formal and by curving them in various directions.

FLOWER CENTRES
For the centres of the flowers, pipe a bulb of icing in a contrasting colour, then allow to dry. If required, pipe on tiny spikes or bulbs of icing using tube (tip) No. 0 or 00, with suitably coloured royal icing.

Opposite: These small flowers are easily piped using the pressure piping technique. Form the petals by piping heart shapes in groups of four or more, a coloured bulb depicts the stamens. Leaves can be piped as pulled dots.

PETAL DUSTING POWDER
Edible coloured petal dusting powder can be used effectively to add more interest and detail to the flowers. Apply petal dust to dry petals using a soft brush before the centre of the flower is piped.

PIPED FLOWERS USING A FLOWER NAIL

Using one basic tube (tip) No. 57, 58 or 59 (the difference being the size), which are available in right-handed and left-handed versions, a flower or rose nail and small squares of waxed paper about 2.5 cm (1 inch) square, a whole host of blooms can be produced. Basic symmetrical flowers such as the daisy and primrose can be achieved through to more detailed ones with overlapping and various sized petals, such as the sweet pea and pansy.

Provided they are kept dry, piped flowers can be made well in advance and stored in boxes between layers of tissue paper. Why not make a selection of piped flowers as a standby for that last-minute cake?

The nail (used for any flower, not just roses) is used as a mini turntable to rotate between your finger and thumb to control its movement. Piping perfect flowers does take practise; as with other forms of piping the technique is based on the regulation of the pressure.

CONSISTENCY OF ICING
The royal icing used to pipe flowers needs to be fairly firm, so that the petals retain their shape when piped and until dry. Beat the icing to almost a full peak (see page 15), adding a few drops of lemon juice or a pinch of cream of tartar. This will produce a good strong icing that will set firm.

Prepare the piping bag, insert the tube (tip), then two-thirds fill with icing. Fold the top over to seal. Pipe a tiny dab of icing on to the flower nail and attach a waxed paper square; I usually press the icing on the flat of the nail then on to a waxed paper square to pick it up.

PROFESSIONAL TIP
Try piping flowers on to a folded square of waxed paper and allow them to dry. The resulting flower will have a natural curve.

PROFESSIONAL TIP
An alternative to the lemon juice or cream of tartar is the addition of a few drops of acetic acid, available for food use from the chemist (drug store).

Above: Deep cup flower nails are now widely available. They are used for lilies and poinsettia (see page 80).

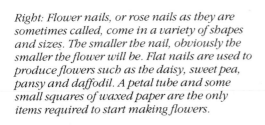

Right: Flower nails, or rose nails as they are sometimes called, come in a variety of shapes and sizes. The smaller the nail, obviously the smaller the flower will be. Flat nails are used to produce flowers such as the daisy, sweet pea, pansy and daffodil. A petal tube and some small squares of waxed paper are the only items required to start making flowers.

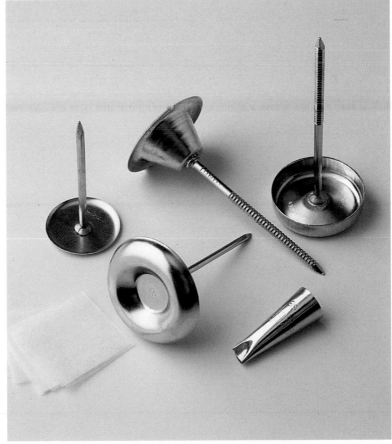

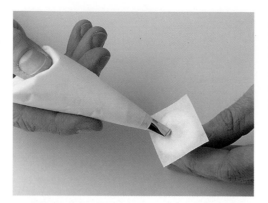

1 Resting the tube on the nail.

Step 1

Holding the piping bag firmly, rest the tube on the nail, the wider end of the tube should always be towards the centre of the flower, so that the thinner end creates the fine edge of the petal when piped.

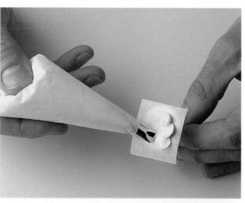

2 Piping a tight horseshoe shape.

Step 2

Start piping, apply pressure to the bag to extrude the icing then, at the same time, rotate the flower nail very slightly and pipe a tight 'horseshoe' shape. Release the pressure as you return back to the centre of the flower, twisting your wrist to create the curve of the petal. Rotate the flower nail ready to position the tube for piping the next petal. Repeat the same procedure for piping the first petal.

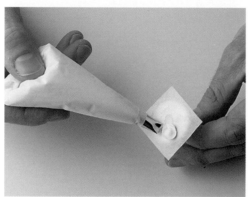

3 Piping the third petal.

Step 3

Rotate the flower nail and pipe a third petal. You should have covered half the circumference of the flower, if not the petals are either too wide or too narrow.

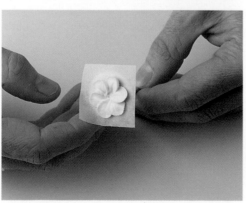

4 Removing the completed flower.

Step 4

Repeat the first three steps to pipe the remaining three petals, releasing the tube carefully after the last petal is complete. Pipe a small dot or bulb into the centre of the flower using a contrasting colour of icing to complete a basic blossom flower.

For the blossom and all flowers, remove the flower from the nail as soon as piping is complete. Carefully place the flowers on a work board or cake board and set aside in a dry place until required for use on the cake.

DAISY

Use the same technique as described for a basic blossom but create elongated horseshoe shapes to make long narrow petals, piping a total of ten petals. Allow the flower to dry, then pipe in a yellow green coloured bulb of royal icing. Gently place the flower into yellow coloured caster (superfine) sugar. Lift the flower from the sugar, then remove any excess caster sugar to reveal an attractive centre for the daisy. Brush with petal dusting powder, if liked.

BESS ROSE

Prepare the piping bag and insert the tube (tip), then fill with white icing down one side of the bag and a pale pink down the other to create a tonal effect as shown. Place the pink colour down the side of the bag with the narrow end of the tube, so that the colour is on the edge of the petals when piped. The technique is similar to the basic blossom, but half-way through piping each of the four petals, quickly move the tube back and forth to make a heart shape.

To finish the rose, lightly colour the centre with edible green coloured petal dusting powder. Finally, pipe a group of egg-yellow coloured royal icing bulbs to form the cluster of stamen.

DAFFODIL

Base this flower on the basic blossom technique, piping six petals. The difference being that as soon as the six petals are completed and before the icing starts to set, use a slightly moistened brush to pull out each petal to a pointed shape.

For the trumpet of the flower, pipe in a circular fashion using a No. 2 tube (tip). Finish the edge of the trumpet by piping a fine line of orange coloured icing using a No. 1 or 0 tube. Alternatively, allow the trumpet to dry, then paint the orange detail with food colouring using a fine paint brush.

NARCISSUS

Pipe the narcissus like the Daffodil but in white icing. Finish the edge of the trumpet with a fine line of orange coloured icing, either pipe or paint on.

Daisy.

Bess rose.

Daffodil.

Narcissus.

Pansy.

Christmas rose.

Primrose.

Sweet pea.

PANSY

Prepare the piping bag with two colours as for the Bess Rose method. Use yellows, violets, blues etc or simply use one colour and add further detail when the flower is finished. Pipe two petals opposite each other as shown, then two slightly larger petals beneath the first two. Finally pipe one fairly large petal opposite the first two, slightly overlapping the bottom two. Finish the flower with a tiny bulb of yellow-orange coloured icing, pulling out to a spike shape. While the flower is still soft, paint very fine lines radiating from the centre to create varying colour schemes.

CHRISTMAS ROSE

This is a five petalled flower, each petal being piped in a similar manner to the Daffodil, where a point is made on the tip of each petal. Make the petals a little wider than the daffodil by applying more pressure. Finish with a light tint of pale green petal dusting powder to give the characteristic waxy look of this flower. Pipe the centre with yellow coloured icing.

PRIMROSE

This delicate flower has just five petals each the same and piped symmetrically. To make the attractively shaped petal simply move the tube (tip) outwards, then quickly in and out and back to the centre to make a heart shape. Repeat this four times as shown. Finish the flower by colouring the centre with egg-yellow coloured petal dusting powder and pipe in a few tiny pale green coloured dots.

SWEET PEA

The technique for piping sweet peas involves continually moving the tube up and down, and a little back and forth, to form the delicate frill appearance of the petals. Pipe one large petal at the top left. Overlap with a petal of the same size at top right. Next pipe a large wide petal to cover the bases of the two petals. Finally hold the bag almost upright and pipe a bulbous leaf shape. Using stem green coloured royal icing and a No. 1 or 2 tube (tip), pipe the calyx and a bulb. The bulb is the part to attach to the end of the stem when arranging the flowers.

You can use the two colour icing method described for Bess Rose; although pink, lilac or rose coloured petal dusting powder applied to the petal edges looks equally attractive.

ROSE

The rose is probably the most popular flower used in cake decoration. For this, the piping bag is held so that the tube (tip) is standing up, with the wide end of the tube at the base and the curved thin end pointing outwards to assist in forming the correct shape of the petals. Pipe a rose on a cocktail stick (toothpick), removing the stick before using.

Step 1

Start with a central cone, rotating the cocktail stick as you pipe. Allow to dry, making subsequent piping easier and the flower will retain a better shape.

Step 2

Next pipe two vertical petals tucking the second one into the first, allow to dry.

Step 3

Finally pipe three petals to form a full rose, each one being tucked into the previous one. Pipe the larger outer petals in a lightly frilled horseshoe shape using a combination of the blossom and sweet pea piping movements.

Tonal effects to the petals can be achieved by using the two colour icing method (see Bess Rose) or by applying edible coloured petal dusting powder.

For buds, simply pipe the central cone and pipe on a calyx using green icing.

Once completely dry, the icing roses can be attractively arranged with piped leaves as shown to form a beautiful centrepiece for a cake. The use of dusting powder lightly brushed on the edges of the petals provides realism.

1 First pipe a central cone.

2 Pipe two vertical petals.

3 Pipe three full petals to finish.

DEEP FLOWER NAILS

As well as the traditional flat flower nail, there are other deep cup flower nails commercially available. These deep flower nails can be used to produce flowers with deep centres and curving petals. Lilies are an ideal bloom to pipe on this nail, ideally suited for the long stamen which is inserted while the icing is soft.

Lightly grease the deep cup with white fat first. When dry, release the flower by holding the nail under a gentle warmth while carefully twisting the flower.

PIPING LEAVES

For most floral decoration, leaves are usually required to complete the arrangement. A selection of popular leaf shapes and combinations can be seen below, all of which are piped using a special leaf piping tube (tip). If you do not have a leaf tube, you can cut a shaped aperture (see page 54) from a conventional paper piping bag. This would be suitable for only a few leaves as the end of the bag becomes moist and the leaf veining and shape gets distorted.

With both 'tubes', the method of piping is simply to vary the pressure and 'jerk' the bag a little as you pipe to form the vein detail.

Right: Using flowers to decorate a cake will undoubtedly require some form of leaves, stems and foliage to complement them. The holly leaves (far right) are piped and then pulled out with a fine paint brush.

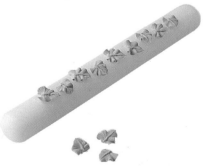

Above: To make leaves with more natural curves to them, pipe them on to a rolling pin covered with waxed paper. Allow the leaves to dry, then carefully remove as required.

To make coloured sugar for the centres of flowers, mix paste or liquid colour into caster (superfine) sugar and then spread on a baking tray to dry completely before use.

Piped flowers can be incorporated into a cake design in many different ways, they do however look most attractive when combined with stems and foliage to form a feature decoration. Choose leaves that suit the flower best, for botanically correct matching, refer to a gardening book.

For a violet, use a deep violet coloured icing and a tiny petal tube (tip) made from a No. 4 tube (tip), shaped using fine pointed nosed pliers. Pipe two large petals opposite each other, then two narrower petals beneath them. Finally, pipe a large petal at the base. A spike of orange-yellow coloured icing completes the flower.

LETTERING

You will no doubt agree that lettering can be one of the most difficult aspects of cake decoration – if you let it! There are various ways of successfully adding words to your cakes. To start with, select the lettering method that suits your own level of ability, enabling you to eventually progress as you learn to the more intricate and advanced techniques.

BLUE JAZZ CAKE

Something different such as this triangular shaped cake makes an exciting change from the conventional round and square shapes. The star lines are made on waxed paper and attached to the cake when dry. Make the saxophone as a runout and paint with gold colour. The stars are stencilled and then painted silver.

Many hours of painstaking work are usually spent creating a special cake, only to be spoiled by the lettering. It may be that the letters are not spaced correctly, or that the word is sloping to one side of the cake top, or even that the style chosen is unsuitable for the occasion.

Although it may seem easier to use just flowers or figures, painted plaques and so on to decorate your cakes, there is a great sense of achievement and enjoyment to be had when writing in icing. You can accomplish a total look to your cakes by the addition of an appropriate inscription or greeting.

The main points to bear in mind when considering lettering for cakes are: style, size, colour, spacing and position.

STYLE

Select a lettering style which is suited to either the occasion or the recipient of the cake, or both. A good example of a style that suits the occasion is the popular Old English style lettering used to complement a traditional festive scene on a Christmas cake.

Suiting the style to the recipient can be more difficult, for instance a child's or elderly person's cake should ideally carry lettering that is legible and easily recognizable. Here you would use fairly simple, bold and uncluttered lettering, probably in bright attractive colours for the child and more subtle pastel colours for the older person.

Directly piped lettering lends itself particularly well to embellishing with extra colour, decorative lines and dots and of course serifs and 'curly' ends to the last letter of a word or name. A few examples are illustrated here in both capitals and lower case letters along with an attractive script style.

SIZE

Making the lettering the correct size is important, although there are no rules about this. It is all a matter of visual appeal and that the lettering looks 'comfortable' on the cake. You will be able to tell as you progress by your own experience. If the inscription or name overpowers the rest of the decoration then it is too big, alternatively if it looks tiny and lost then it must be too small. Try to strike a happy medium between the cake top border (piped or runout collar), the decoration (flowers, figures) and the overall space remaining which is allocated to the lettering, all three should complement each other.

COLOUR

The choice of colour for the lettering plays an important part in the design and overall appearance of a cake. Badly coloured lettering can often spoil rather than improve or complement a design if not used with care. The basic colour schemes described in *Cake Design* will provide a guide to the choice of colour for a particular design.

A point to note when applying coloured lettering, especially for those new to this aspect of decoration, is that it is wise to first pipe the lettering in the same colour (base colour) as the iced surface. In this way, if a mistake is made, the lines can be carefully lifted off with a fine paint brush. Having mastered the inscription in base colour, it is then easier for beginners to overpipe with confidence in colour.

Various options for coloured lettering can be considered:

Using the same colour in a slightly stronger tint.

Using a stronger colour.

Using a matching colour.

USING THE SAME COLOUR
The lettering can be worked in the same colour. This is standard practice for most commercial work and indeed for a particular design where the lettering should not look fussy or detract from other decoration on the cake.

USING A STRONGER COLOUR
The main or most important part of the inscription or message, such as the name or age of a person or anniversary, could be made to stand out from the rest by using a stronger colour. The greeting therefore could be in a paler tint than the name, or use two or more completely different colours of icing.

USING MATCHING COLOUR
The colour of the lettering could be one that has already been used elsewhere in

Far Left: Using a different colour.

Left: White lettering on white icing.

the design, such as the colour of line often used to overpipe linework or a piped border. You may even like to match the lettering to the ribbon used on the cake or to the colours in a floral arrangement or modelled top ornament.

USING A DIFFERENT COLOUR

Use a colour completely different to any already used on the cake to make it really stand out from everything else. Dark brown or chocolate coloured lettering always stands out well and, providing it is neatly piped, does look crisp and clean on most colour schemes. Take great care when using strong colours that the tube is reasonably fine, otherwise the greeting or inscription will be overpowering.

Lettering in the same colour as the icing used to coat the cake can look quite effective, for instance a white cake with lettering piped on in white, particularly attractive on anniversary cakes and festive cakes. This type of lettering is subtly attractive, being seen clearly only by the shadows cast from it on to the cake surface. Do not use an extremely fine tube for this application as it will probably be difficult to read the finished inscription.

SPACING

Spacing is probably the most important aspect of lettering, even the best piped letters forming a name or inscription can look entirely disjointed if the spacing is incorrect. The rule to employ is **not** to space the letters equally, but to space them visually to appear with equal intervals between each letter. The example shows a word with equal spacing between each letter. The same word is also shown with the letters spaced correctly (not evenly) so as to appear with an equal interval of space between.

Equal amounts of space between each letter.

Letters with varying amounts of space between to appear evenly spaced.

POSITION

The actual positioning of the lettering within an allocated space on the cake top does require some thought and care. Do not place all the decoration, such as the figure or flowers, and the lettering together in one area of the cake top. Try to produce a pleasing balance so that there is a feeling of space. Also take care not to position the lettering (or decoration) too near the cake edge.

METHODS OF APPLICATION

There are various ways to actually apply the lettering to the iced surface of your cake. Some are more intricate and advanced, so select the method that suits your level of ability and then progress to the other techniques later.

DIRECTLY PIPED

This method as its name implies is carried out by piping straight and curved lines from a fine writing tube directly on to the iced surface of the cake or plaque, producing individual letters, making words or inscriptions. This technique is also used for the traditional script lettering. The basic directly piped lettering can be overpiped in various ways and with other colours to provide some really interesting effects and combinations.

Piped lettering employs exactly the same techniques as linework piping, so before attempting to pipe any lettering at all, it is advisable to first read *Linework*. This will give you a better understanding of tube (tip) handling and how to simultaneously control pressure and speed when piping.

Overpiping on directly piped lettering.

First practise on a plastic sheet, cake board or similar. You can then keep wiping the practice lettering off until you perfect the style.

Transfer the chosen lettering style on to the cake by pin-pricking or tracing (see page 64), then follow the letters using the basic piping sequence in *Templates*. You can use the sequence guide to assist you with most basic lettering styles. Until you become more proficient, the joins in each letter may require neatening with a fine, moistened paint brush.

Pin-pricking lettering on to the icing.

Piping the lettering.

The finished lettering.

Piping the lettering.

Overpiping in a different colour.

The finished lettering.

1 Outlining the lettering by piping.   *2 Flooding-in the outlined lettering.*   *3 Leaving to dry before removing.*

RUNOUT
Runout lettering uses the same basic technique described in *Runout Work*.

Step 1
Place a piece of plastic film or waxed paper over a template of the lettering style chosen. Using a No. 0 or 1 tube (tip), outline the lettering.

Step 2
Flood-in the outline with runout consistency icing (see page 91) and allow to dry.

Step 3
Once dry, the individual letters can be carefully removed from the backing and attached to the cake with small dabs of royal icing.

ILLUMINATED
Not truly a technique, more a style involving a combination of two or more techniques. Sometimes known as embellished lettering, excellent examples of which can be found in religious books and on old manuscripts. It is very popular to embellish or incorporate extra decoration to the first or capital letter of a word, greeting or inscription. As can be seen from the photograph, the basis of the embellishment can be stencilled, runout or directly piped. The additional lines of the letter can then be directly piped as for the remaining letters of the name or word.

STENCILLED
This is a very quick and relatively easy method of applying lettering to the cake. The basic technique of cutting and using a stencil is described in *Stencilling*. Here are some examples of stencilled lettering that can be applied directly to cake tops or on to prefabricated plaques, producing simple yet effective results.

PREFABRICATED PLAQUES
This method is probably one of the easiest methods to use for the first time cake decorator. The plaque is prepared with the appropriate lettering off the cake. It is then simply attached to the iced surface with small dabs of icing. These plaques can be made of royal icing, using the runout technique, to prepare attractive shapes.

Illuminated letters.

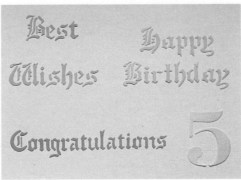

Stencilled letters.

Right: Using a small plaque for each letter.

Far Right: Numerals of various designs.

Having prepared a suitable plaque, add the lettering to it using one or more of the described techniques. Choose a lettering to suit the cake and your ability.

NUMERALS

All the numerals illustrated can be made using the same basic principles for lettering and inscriptions.

MONOGRAMS

These consist of two or more initial letters intertwined to form a motif. Their most popular use is for the side panels of wedding cakes to feature the bride and groom's initials. First make individual tracings of the letters required, then overlap them and move them around in varying configurations until well positioned.

Step 3

Allow each section to dry before filling in an adjacent section or different colour.

MONOGRAM FINISHES

● Outline with a contrasting or complementary colour to the flood-in colour.
● Outline with icing, then allow to dry. Carefully paint the outline with edible silver or gold colouring. Flood-in with suitably coloured runout icing and dry.
● Outline and flood-in with icing, then allow to dry. When dry, paint the monogram with edible silver or gold colouring.
● Outline and flood-in the monogram with the same colour icing, then dry. Shade from the top or from the base with a tint of a suitable colour to create a faded effect. The shading can be applied using petal dusting powder or an airbrush.

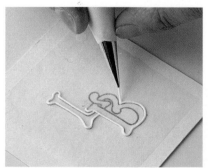

Step 1

Make a tracing of the monogram and place a piece of waxed paper or plastic film over the top, securing with masking tape or a few dabs of royal icing. Outline the monogram by piping.

Step 2

Follow the technique described for runout lettering, flooding-in small sections at a time.

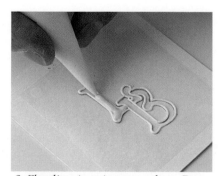

1 Outlining the monogram by piping.

2 Flooding-in using one colour. Dry.

3 Flooding-in using a different colour.

Monograms make a special feature to any wedding cake and look most attractive positioned on the side of say the base tier; they also make the cake more personalized to the bride and groom. Here are a few variations on the basic theme including the use of gold and silver colour, colour shading and outlining in a darker colour.

RUNOUT WORK

Spectacular runout work has become more and more popular over the years. It is mostly associated with runout collars, these are prefabricated off-pieces (made using the runout technique) used to decorate cakes. Runout collars are attached to the top surface of the cake and extend over the edge, thus increasing the border area and giving the cake an appearance of being larger than it actually is. A border in the form of a runout to match the top design is sometimes

FILIGREE AND FLOWERS 21ST CAKE

Runout collars are used extensively on royal iced cakes but rarely are they given any extra decoration. This idea of piping delicate filigree work with a fine tube (tip) *over the collars provides a soft, feminine look to the cake. Piped flowers and ribbon loops add subtle interest to this beautiful cake. (See* Templates.*)*

repeated around the base as an alternative to a directly piped border.

Other decorative runout items include figures, plaques, centrepieces, models, numerals and lettering.

Runout work is the principle of outlining (although outlines are not always necessary) a given shape with piping consistency icing using a fine tube (tip), usually on to waxed paper, plastic film or special runout film. The outlined shape is then flooded-in with an albumen or water softened royal icing (run-icing), through a small aperture in a paper piping bag. Having flooded the shape, the runout piece is then dried in a gentle heat to produce a semi-glossy, dried piece. The runout is then removed from the backing material, by peeling off the waxed paper or film. Prepared runout pieces are attached to the cake with icing.

Similar 'rules' apply to all runout work, it is simply the template or use of the runout piece that will vary. Once you understand the principles of this aspect of royal icing work, you can then adapt it more readily to your individual requirements.

PREPARATION

Good preparation is definitely one of the key factors of successful runout work. Problems always occur when you start piping only to have to leave off and find a paint brush or scissors or some other piece of essential equipment. Use the informative materials checklist below each time you start any runout work until you get into your own routine of working.

MATERIALS
Royal icing (piping consistency – see page 15) for outlining
Albumen or water for diluting icing
Small mixing bowl
Edible food colours (if required)
Greaseproof paper piping bags
Piping tube (tip) No. 1
Work board (wooden or plastic)
Waxed paper/plastic film/runout sheet
Masking tape
Scissors
Fine paint brush
Small bladed palette knife
Small craft knife
Angled reading or desk lamp

TEMPLATES
Ensure that the templates and patterns used are completely flat (no lumps of dried icing from a previous use), otherwise the runout shape will dry unevenly. Make sure the template is of a manageable size – do not have a tiny drawing on a large sheet of paper, cut off any excess before starting to pipe. (See also *Templates.*)

WAXED PAPER/PLASTIC FILM
Cut the waxed paper sufficiently large enough to cover the template area, this makes piping easier and reduces wasted waxed paper. Also ensure that the paper is free of creases.

MAKING RUN-ICING

Use fresh royal icing made up to normal piping consistency (see page 15). Stored icing becomes very heavy, moist and glossy and will produce dull, crumbly runout pieces. If the icing is very heavy, very lightly re-beat it for a few seconds before use.

Place the required amount of icing in a bowl and thin it out with a small amount of water or albumen. Using albumen for thinning down will produce stronger runouts with a better surface sheen, than using water. Add the extra liquid a little at a time until you achieve the correct consistency. Stir the icing, do not beat while incorporating the liquid. Beating the mixture will produce air bubbles in the icing.

To judge the correct consistency of the icing, lift the spoon and form a ribbon of

Attaining the correct consistency of run-icing is crucial to good runout work. The icing should run back into itself finding its own level at the count of ten.

icing across the bowl. Slowly counting to ten, the icing should just run back into itself (all ripples subsided) as you reach ten. Cover with a clean damp cloth and use as soon as possible. Do not store mixed run-icing for later use, always use it immediately after thinning.

Many tutors and text books often advise leaving the prepared run-icing to stand to let the bubbles subside before using it. Really there should not be any need to do this. You should be able to start using the icing immediately, providing you do not overbeat the icing at the liquid addition stage and that the aperture cut in the piping bag is not too large.

Spoon just sufficient run-icing into a piping bag; do not overfill. A piping tube (tip) is not required for flooding-in, instead using scissors cut a neat hole at the point of the bag no larger than the size of a No. 2 tube. If the hole is cut too large, then the bubbles escape and find their way into the actual runout piece. These eventually end up as grey spots on the dry surface. You can actually tell when the hole is the correct size because you will hear the bubbles 'bursting' as they are forced from the bag, through the hole and into the runout piece.

It is important to dry runouts as quickly as possible near a gentle source of heat, in order to obtain a good surface sheen and firm shape. A desk or reading lamp with a flexible arm is ideal for this.

Outlining and Flooding-in

Step 1

Trace the template on to cartridge paper and cut out. Place the template on to the work board you intend to dry the finished runout on. Place a suitably sized piece of waxed paper or plastic film over the drawing or design, remember no creases and not too big. Secure with tiny dabs of icing at the corners or small pieces of masking tape. Do not use drawing pins to secure your paper, this can result in accidents and damaged runouts. Outline the shape by piping on to the waxed paper or plastic film using a No. 1 tube (tip) and piping consistency icing.

1 Outlining the runout shape by piping.

Release the paper or plastic from the icing dabs or masking tape and carefully remove the template from beneath, taking care not to damage the piped outline. Alternatively, the template may be removed after flooding-in – decide for yourself when you find it easiest to remove the template.

Step 2

Cut a No. 2 size aperture off the end of the prepared piping bag of run-icing. Use sharp scissors to make a neat cut. Flood-in the outline, usually piping around the inside edge of the outline first. Using a side-to-side movement, evenly flood-in the shape with icing. Do not overfill the shape, otherwise the icing

2 Flooding-in the outlined shape.

may come over the outline. At the same time, do not under-fill as this creates a fragile runout, with an uneven surface.

Step 3

In the case of detailed outlines, such as this scalloped edge, use a fine paint brush to assist the flow of the run-icing into the outline edge. The paint brush can also be used to prick any air bubbles that may appear (if the hole in the bag was too large) on the surface of the runout shape.

If the icing has not flowed out evenly, this can be encouraged by sliding a thin bladed knife under the waxed paper or film and moving it gently from side-to-side.

Step 4

Using small pieces of masking tape, secure the runout piece to the board, again making sure that the waxed paper or film is perfectly flat – the way you leave it is the way it will dry! Immediately after flooding-in is completed, place the runout under a gentle source of heat and allow it to dry completely. Use a desk or

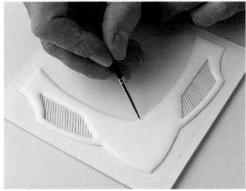

3 With a brush, moving icing to the edge.

reading lamp with a flexible arm over the icing (or other gentle heat source) to help it to 'crust' over rapidly and ensure a good gloss. Under no circumstances, for safety reasons, should you place the work near a naked flame. If the runout shape is **not** placed in heat, the surface will sink and have a dull appearance.

PROFESSIONAL TIP
Broken runout collars can sometimes be rescued by joining from the back with royal icing supported by some waxed paper, which can be removed later.

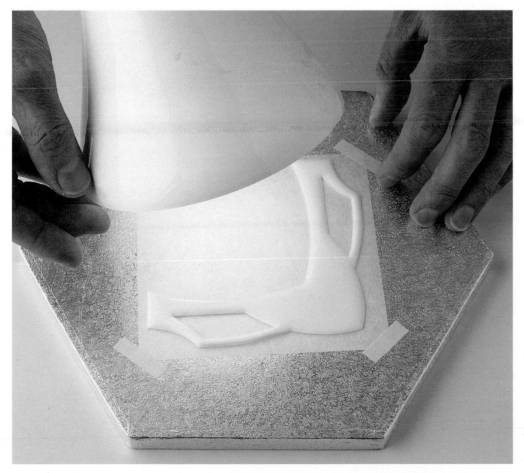

4 There are a few different methods of drying runouts, the one most widely used is a gentle heat source from a desk lamp with a flexible arm as shown. The most important point is to crust the icing surface as quickly as possible after flooding-in, and then to continue drying to prevent the icing sinking.

MAKING LARGE RUNOUTS AND FULL COLLARS

For larger runout pieces, such as full collars, the technique varies a little. The collar runout example shown is a full collar, suitable for a round cake. However the method described is used for other shapes, such as hexagonal, oval, petal and the square cake collar design opposite, which has a fairly detailed outline shape and cut-out sections.

Place the prepared template on a board and cover with a suitably sized piece of waxed paper, plastic film or runout film, securing with dots of icing or masking tape at each corner.

Outline the shape by piping using a No. 1 tube (tip). Carefully remove the template from beneath the waxed paper

To prevent unsightly joins when producing large runout pieces and full collars in particular, it is advisable to employ this flooding-in sequence described below.

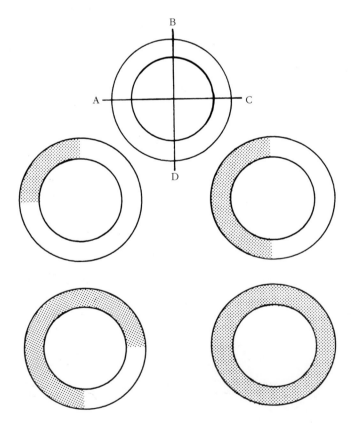

or plastic film (or leave until after flooding-in).

Flood-in the shape – this is where the technique varies, because the flooding is over a larger area. If the flooding-in is started and finished at the same place, the run-icing at the start of the flooding-in will probably be slightly crusted over by the time you reach it to complete the shape. This will result in an unsightly join, due to the crusted icing cracking and not blending with the soft icing. To overcome this problem, follow this method:

Start flooding at point A, then flood to point B.
Return to point A, then flood to point D.
Return to point B, then flood to point C.
Finally flood-in the last section from point D to point C. Using this method, no section has a chance to crust before being merged with more run-icing, therefore no joins will be visible.

Use a paint brush to perfect any fine detail. Secure the runout shape to the board, ensuring the paper is taut and free from creases.

Finally, before setting large runouts aside to dry, make (cut) a cross in the centre of the waxed paper or plastic film with a craft knife, this will assist in retaining a flat runout piece and prevent warping. Sometimes as the moist run-icing dries it causes tension on the paper, and becomes distorted, the cut in the paper or film prevents this occurring.

DRYING RUNOUTS

Drying runout work is often a matter of trial and error to find out your own most successful method. You can use a desk or reading lamp with a flexible arm, a cool oven with the oven door slightly ajar to let moisture escape, and purpose made drying cabinets using light bulbs as a source of heat.

The aim is to allow the moisture in the icing to evaporate and eventually dry to a brittle solid finish. Keep the pieces away from moisture and steam, even when they have dried completely.

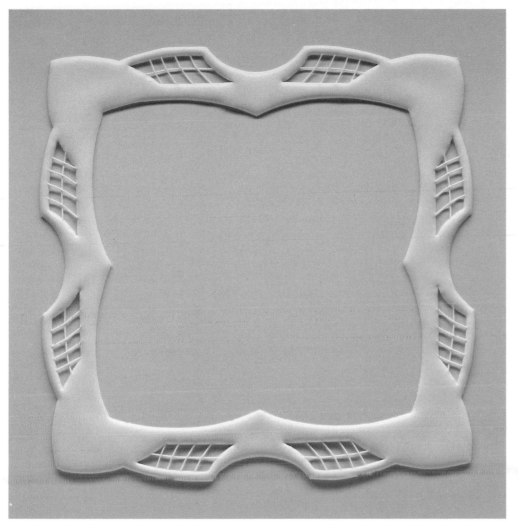

PROFESSIONAL TIP
Base collars can be made in sections to be positioned around the cake or the full collar attached to the coated board and the cake positioned inside it. Alternatively, the full collar can be placed over the cake and down on to the cake board.

Using the flooding-in sequence described on the opposite page will result in a perfect runout with no unsightly joins and a good even shape. Detail in the cut-outs can be piped in at the outlining stage or you may prefer to make the collar, allow it to dry and then add the detail piping.

BASE COLLARS

Illustrated below are four different methods that can be employed when decorating a cake with base collars. The first method is described on page 146.

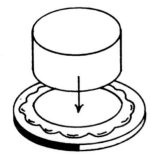

Attach the collar to the cake board and lower the cake down.

Outline and flood-in the collar directly on to the cake board.

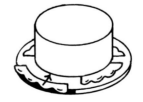

Make the collar in separate sections and attach as shown.

Make the runout collar and lower it over the cake on to the board.

TYPES OF COLLARS

QUARTER OR CORNER COLLAR

These, as the name suggests, are made four to a cake. Quarter collars for round cakes and corner collars for square ones. They can be used with linework piped adjacent to them, incorporating the space between them within the design. Or small overlays (opposite) may be used to conceal the spaces and give the appearance of a full collar. These are the most manageable collars to make as they are easy to handle and can be adjusted to fit the cake.

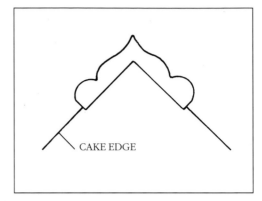

SIDE COLLAR

A full side collar gives enormous scope for further creative design, being an alternative to corner collars, they are still sectional and have four corner spaces. Use these spaces to advantage to incorporate complementary decoration when planning your design.

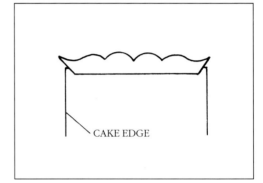

COLLAR SECTIONS

Again similar to both corners and side collars but usually smaller. This type of collar lends itself particularly well to multi-sided cakes such as hexagonal and octagonal shapes. The spaces between each section can be decorated or covered with a small overlay.

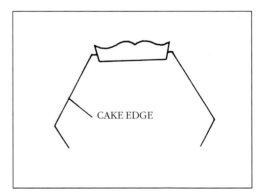

FULL COLLAR

A complete 'band' or border of icing to fit around the top edge or base of a cake.

Note Always make spare runout collar pieces in case of any breakages. For small sections or corners, make one extra, for example make five for a square cake or seven for a hexagonal shaped cake. If making a full collar, you will need to make two.

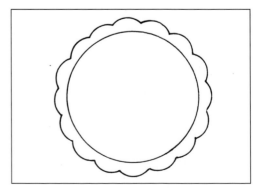

ADDITIONAL COLLAR SECTIONS

To make a basic runout collar more interesting or improve the detail, you may occasionally want to try some of the following effects. However, do not over-do the extra work, far better to produce a classic runout collar without too much gimmicky embellishment.

UNDER COLLARS
A collar with a slightly larger inside measurement to that of the top collar is positioned to show a contrasting or complementary colour or a decorative texture.

OVERLAYS
These can be small sections to conceal joins on quarter and corner collars or narrow width full collars that rest on another collar. The overlay can be plain, textured or patterned.

CUT-OUT SECTIONS

Some collar designs lend themselves to opening up a little to make them more airy and delicate. Cut-outs can be incorporated into almost all collar designs both full and sectional, a few examples can be found in *Templates*. Having made the runout you can further decorate the cut-outs with one of the ideas below.

PICOT DOT EDGE
This is piped on to the edge of a cut-out of a dry runout collar, and incidentally can also be used to good effect on the outside edge of the collar. Various combinations of dots and colours can be used (see page 66). You may find it easier releasing the collar from the waxed paper or film before piping the dots on to the runout, otherwise they may break off as you peel off the paper.

SCROLL WORK
Pipe this design into the cut-out section of a collar at the outlining stage and before flooding-in. Ensure that tiny, neat bulbs anchor the fine scroll work to the outline. Numbers and flowers can also be incorporated into the collar.

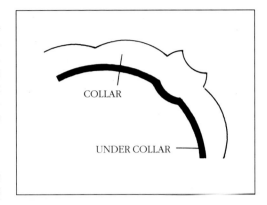

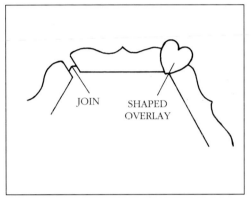

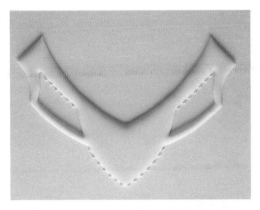

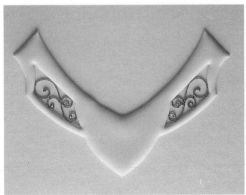

FILIGREE

This can be piped into the cut-out section of a collar at the outline and flooding stage or attached to the dry runout as shown below for line and dot work (see Professional Tip). Filigree also looks attractive when piped on the surface of the collar using a fine tube (tip).

LINE AND DOT

A much used delicate decoration for cut-out sections and often seen on competition cakes. Although it can be piped at the outlining stage, personally I think a far superior finish is obtained using the following technique:

Make the runout collar or sections and allow to dry fully. Before continuing, remove the waxed paper or film backing from the runout.

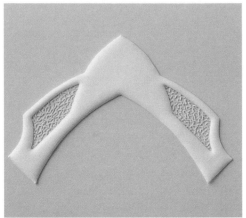
Filigree work.

Step 1

Place a suitably sized piece of waxed paper or plastic film over the prepared template of the line and dot design. Secure the paper with four tiny dabs of icing. Using a fine No. 0 or 1 tube (tip), pipe the lines slightly longer than the template as shown. Pipe a line of icing along the ends of the lines.

PROFESSIONAL TIP
Filigree is a fine line decoration piped using a fine tube (tip) to form a maze of 'M' and 'W' shapes in a continuous but random line over an allocated space.

Step 2

Carefully lift the runout, position it over the lines and align it with the template.

Slide a thin bladed knife between the waxed paper or film and the template and, with slight upward pressure, carefully bond the icing to the runout. Repeat until all the cut-out sections are filled.

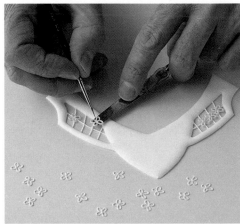
Line and dot work.

Step 3

To add dot work or flowers, re-position the collar over the template and pipe in the required decoration.

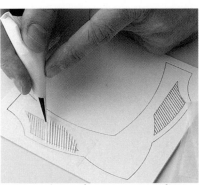
1 Piping lines of icing over template.

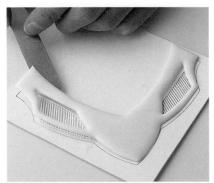
2 Aligning runout over lines.

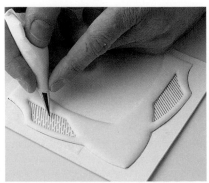
3 Piping dots into linework.

RUNOUT PLAQUES

The runout technique is not restricted to the production of collars for decorating cakes. Plaques in all shapes, sizes and colours can be made using the basic outlining and flooding-in method with an appropriate template. The plaque shapes can be made in advance and stored between layers of tissue paper in a dry place. Plaques are used as bases for cake ornaments, paintings, brush embroidery and lettering.

Eventually you will no doubt want to create your own individual effects. A few to experiment with would be the use of strong coloured outlines to really emphasize the shape of the plaque. You can even paint the piped outline with gold or silver food colouring, prior to flooding-in. Try creating a marbled effect by flooding-in the plaque with white run-icing and, while still wet, pipe on a few dabs of coloured icing. Gently swirl the icing with a cocktail stick (toothpick).

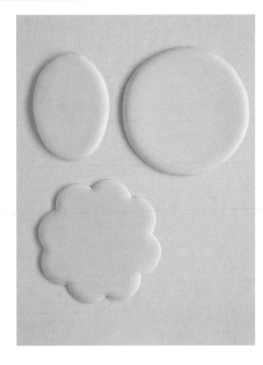

Plaques can be made in many shapes, sizes and colours.

RABBIT RUNOUT FIGURE

Figures and animals are used extensively by cake decorators as centrepieces for cake designs. The technique of outlining and flooding-in with run-icing lends itself ideally to the production of such motifs. This rabbit illustrates a variation of the conventional method of outlining and flooding-in with the same colour of icing. Here, brown coloured icing is used to create a bold outline for the main colour of the rabbit. The detail can be painted on or piped when the runout shape is dry. The finished rabbit figure can be seen on a cake on page 140.

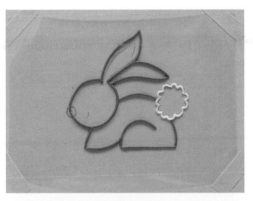

A darker colour icing is used for a bolder outline.

The rabbit figure is flooded-in with a lighter colour.

PRESSURE PIPING

This is a traditional method of piping icing through tubes (tips) to produce ornate three-dimensional figures and pictures, by increasing or decreasing the amount of pressure on the piping bag.

Pressure piped work can be iced directly on to the top or side of the cake, or it can be piped on waxed paper or plastic film and allowed to dry. The dry shapes can then be used as they are or painted and mounted on to plaques.

After practising pressure piping you will no doubt be able to pipe many shapes and figures free-hand. In the early stages though, it may be easier for you to first transfer the design, see page 64.

WHITE SATIN BRIDE CAKE

This elegant single tier bride cake employs many different royal icing skills such as coating, piping, runout work and linework. The centrepiece is a runout plaque finished with a lily of the valley design piped on using the pressure piping technique. White satin ribbon with flowers and fern completes the decoration.

TUBES (TIPS)

Depending upon the size of the figure or shape to be piped, select a suitably sized piping tube (tip). Two-thirds fill a piping bag with freshly made, well beaten, full peak icing.

Some shapes and figures will require two or more different sized tubes, for instance to pipe the main shape, then to add other details. You will probably need tube No. 4, 3, 2, 1, with possibly 0 and 00.

COLOURS

The shapes can be piped first and then the colour painted on them. Alternatively, the different colours can be piped directly on to the cake, using several bags each with different colours and tube (tip) sizes. Make a note of the colours you are likely to need and prepare them ready,

placing them in a piping bag stand. The following designs are some of the more popular examples of pressure piping used to decorate cakes. Follow the steps to help you learn the technique, then you can try adapting your own designs for pressure piping.

HEARTS
The technique for making these is very similar to piped pulled flowers on page 74. Simply apply pressure to pipe a small plain shell shape with the point facing towards yourself. Immediately and before the icing starts to crust, pipe exactly the same shape alongside the first one to just merge and join, finishing with both ends forming one point. Various sizes can be piped using larger tubes.

LOVER'S KNOT
Using a small tube such as No. 1 or 2, pipe the ribbon loops using varying pressure, piping each loop separately as shown. The tails can then be added, pipe them with naturally flowing curves. The ends of the tails may be left plain or made into a pointed 'v' shape by piping an extra point on to the piped tail and blending both together using a fine paint brush. A small bulb in the centre represents the knot.

DAISY
Using a similar technique to hearts, pipe long slim petal shapes in a formation to produce a round flower shape. These can be piped flat on to waxed paper, or use a flower nail. With experience you can pipe them directly on to the iced surface or runout collar or plaque. When dry, lightly tint the tips of the flower with pale green coloured petal dusting powder. Pipe a yellow bulb in the centre.

LOVE BIRDS

Prepare the wings for the birds in advance, allowing them to dry completely. Pipe left and right wings on to waxed paper using a No.1 tube (tip) with a template.

Using the No. 2 tube pipe a round bulb for the head. Then pipe a bulb shape that tapers to a point to form the body. Pipe the tail using a No. 1 tube. While the icing is still soft, remove a prepared wing from the waxed paper and insert into the body of the bird at an angle. A tiny beak is piped using a No. 0 tube. The eye can be piped or painted on.

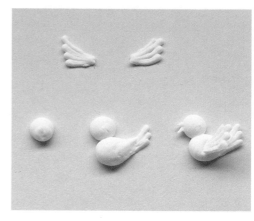

LOVE BIRDS AND DAISY CHAIN

These dainty little birds will enhance celebration cakes of all kinds, in particular wedding cakes. They look most attractive as a decoration for the sides of cakes, especially when incorporated with other features such as flowers, bows, daisy chains and wedding rings. The most accurate method of positioning the birds is to make a template. This can be secured against the cake side while the line and dot work or daisy chain is piped on. Prepared birds are attached to the cake with icing, or you may prefer to pipe them directly on to the cake.

PROFESSIONAL TIP
To adapt your own design, look at the original and decide which part should appear furthest away. Start by piping that part. Build up the shape or figure with the part or parts which appear to be in the 'middle distance'. Now add the parts that appear to be nearest to you and finally pipe on a fine detail to complete the shape.

SWAN

Varying pressure on the piping bag while piping will produce the necessary variations in width as shown here on the neck and body of the swan. Start with the head and neck, then add the body shape. A No. 2 tube (tip) is used to commence building up the wing area, simply outline the shape as shown. Using the same tube, pipe on the tail and wing detail. Finish the swan by piping on the beak with yellow-orange coloured icing. The eye detail can be piped in icing or painted on.

DOG

Different colour combinations of icing can be used for the dog. Pipe the bulbous body shape first, starting at the neck and finishing at the tail. Add the legs, then pipe on the head, controlling the varying pressure to make the pear shape. The muzzle is shown here piped in white and the ears are piped in dark brown coloured icing. Complete the dog with eyes, nose and tail, all piped in icing. Paint on the dots or whiskers on the muzzle.

RABBIT

This is built up in much the same way as the dog. Use varying pressure to form the interestingly shaped body. Pipe over the back and fore legs as shown. Next pipe the oval shaped head and, using a smaller plain tube (tip), vary the pressure to point the ears. Pipe on the nose and tail. Complete the rabbit with the facial details. Paint on the whiskers using a fine paint brush and edible black food colouring.

CHICK

This pressure piped chick is really easy to make and is based on simple drop or button shapes piped on waxed paper. Pipe a large bulb with slightly soft egg-yellow coloured icing. As you pipe, move the tube (tip) to the top left and continue to apply pressure, releasing it gradually so that you form the head of the chick. The technique is shown in two separate stages. Allow to dry, then add texture as for the robin on page 105. Paint in the eye and pipe the feet and beak.

TEDDY BEAR

This charming novelty figure is most useful as a decoration for children's birthday cakes. When piped using delicate tints of pink, blue, lemon or peach, the teddy bear makes an ideal feature for a christening cake or cake for baby's first birthday.

Having prepared the teddy, allow to dry completely. It can be removed from the waxed paper and positioned on the cake or around the cake on the board to appear as if actually sitting up. Alternatively, and as with all pressure piped decorations, when experience is gained the figures can be piped directly on to the cake surface.

First prepare the icing to the colour of your choice, use the colour chart and mixing guide in *Cake Design* as reference. A 'true' teddy type colour as shown here can be made with combinations of orange, brown and egg yellow colour.

For a teddy approximately 2.5 cm (1 inch) high, use a No. 3 tube (tip) for all the piping except the ear outline, which is piped using a No. 2 tube. For smaller or larger figures, decrease or increase the tube size accordingly. Pipe the body as a large oval bulb shape, followed by a round bulb for the head. Pipe the arms and legs by slowly lifting the tube away from the piped body. Pipe two flat bulbs for the ears and overpipe an outline on each ear using the finer tube. When the teddy bear is dry, pipe on the eyes and nose with white and brown icing. The stitching and paws are painted on with black food colouring using a fine paint brush. Add a piped coloured bow tie for extra detail.

BOOTEES

Use a white or a pale colour of icing such as blue, pink or lemon. Pipe the basic bootee shape using a No. 2 tube (tip) as a large tapered bulb as shown, making the toe part quite bulbous and round. Using the same tube, pipe in a circular motion bringing the tube up to make about three or four broken circles on top of each other. Allow the shape to dry. Using a No. 00 tube, pipe delicate filigree in white icing. A prepared piped bow (No. 1 tube) attached completes the decoration.

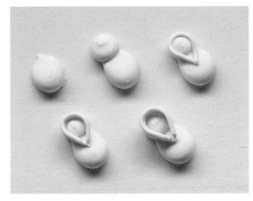

ROBIN

Pipe as for the chick on page 103 using white icing. When the shape is dry, use a fine paint brush to paint on the red breast of the robin – add a little orange colour to the red to make a good bright red. Mix some brown coloured icing with a little water to soften it. Using a small piece of foam sponge, lightly stipple the head and body to add the feather texture to the bird. Using a No. 1 tube (tip), pipe in the eye, legs and beak.

SNOWMAN

This figure decoration is made using a similar principle to the chick and robin as it is based on two flat drop shapes merged together at the piping stage. Allow the shapes to dry, then pipe on the detail as shown. The hat is piped in brown icing using a No. 1 tube (tip). Add a touch of green coloured icing and a few tiny bulbs of red coloured icing for holly and berries. Pipe the facial detail, buttons and scarf using coloured icing.

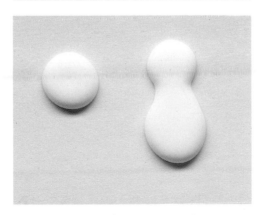

SANTA

Start the basic face shape by piping a flat bulb in semi-soft pinky-peach coloured icing. Allow to dry. Next pipe the hat with red coloured icing, forming it into a tapered point as shown. The beard and moustache is piped using small plain tubes (tips) such as No. 2 or use No. 42 or 43 star tubes to add a little detail in the form of lines. Next pipe the nose, eyes and bobble on the hat. Finish the Santa with a sprig of piped holly and berries in his hat.

Bells painted with gold food colouring.

1 Piping the basic bulb shape.

BELLS

Bells are frequently used as a form of decoration as they can be incorporated into anniversary designs, wedding cakes and of course Christmas and New Year cakes. As well as the flat stencilled type described later in the book, these full-relief piped ones do provide an attractive decoration and can be finished and adapted in several ways.

Step 1

Pipe the basic bulb shape by keeping the piping bag vertical and applying a gentle but even pressure to the icing. Make a round, flat drop or button shape.

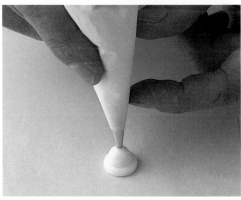

2 Reducing pressure and lifting up.

Step 2

Keeping the tube (tip) in the icing and the piping bag still vertical, continue to pipe but reduce the pressure and at the same time lift the bag upwards. This will form a tapered bell shape as shown.

Step 3

Place the shapes in a gentle heat to crust the surface – the warmth from a desk or reading lamp with a flexible arm is sufficient. Use a fine paint brush to scoop out the soft icing centre, set aside to dry completely before finishing as desired.

If the bell shapes collapse when you try to remove the centre, allow a further short period of drying time.

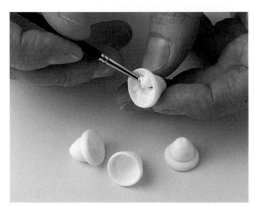

3 Removing soft icing with a paint brush.

Frosted Bells

To make bells with a frosted effect suitable for Christmas cakes and other novelty use, simply sprinkle fine caster (superfine) sugar or coarse granulated sugar over the bells as soon as they are piped and before the icing starts to crust over.

Gold or Silver Bells

To make the basic plain pressure piped bells more attractive, the dried shapes can be painted with gold or silver food colouring as shown. Paint the inside first, enabling you to hold the bell without getting colour on your fingers, then place the bell on waxed paper and paint the outside. Leave the bells just with silver or gold for anniversary cakes, but for Christmas cakes pipe on a little white icing and sprinkle with caster (superfine) sugar to give a frosty effect. When the bells are in position, other decorative piping may be added.

CLOWN

This amusing character will add colour and a sense of fun to novelty and birthday cakes. You can let your imagination run riot with colour and expression – in fact anything goes!

There is really no set design for clowns as you can shape and form the body, legs and arms in various proportions – they are caricatures so proportion isn't that important.

Start by trying the clown figure as shown, you can then experiment with your own ideas. Use tube (tip) No. 3 for all the body, head and limbs, adding finer details using smaller tubes. Pipe the legs by reducing the pressure on the piping bag as you end at the top of the leg. The legs need to be piped first so that the body can overlap the top of the legs. Add the arms, piping in a similar manner as the legs. The head, hands and shoes are piped next in order to be able to cover the joins with the neck, sleeve and trouser ruffle. Complete the clown with piped hat, facial detail and buttons.

STENCILLING

Stencilling has long been associated with the confectioner and commercial cake decorator, used for the quick decoration of gâteaux and celebration cakes. It is probably one of the easiest aspects of cake decoration, at least as far as application is concerned. However, the actual cutting of your own stencil can be quite involved, but once made can be used many times.

There is now commercially available a good range of high quality stencils in various materials, from water resistant stencil card to food grade plastic and stainless steel. All these stencils carry a comprehensive array of designs for different occasions. As a result of these new materials and the creative work of cake decorators seen at exhibitions, stencilling is undergoing a revival.

STORK AND BOW CHRISTENING CAKE

A simple, yet very effective design for a christening cake is provided here by the use of a stencilled stork motif, which features painted detail and shading, see page 114.

The two colour base coating enables the ribbon bows on the cake side to be highlighted against the white. The bows are also stencilled directly on to the cake.

Far Left: Selection of readily available stencils.

Left: Hand-made stencils are easily produced.

A definition of cake stencilling is the art of painting or applying coloured icing through openings on a sheet of strong paper, metal or plastic, so that the impression is left on the surface, in this case royal icing, underneath. All stencils are developments of this basic process, as the technique of application is the same whatever the design.

In addition to flat stencilling of food colouring or icing on to a prepared surface, stencilled pieces can also be formed on curved shapes and left to dry. The dried, prefabricated pieces can then be assembled to make flowers, waterlilies, butterflies and so on (see pages 111–112).

With careful choice of a design and good preparation of the stencil with intricate detail, it is quite often difficult to detect that a stencil has been used to produce the multi-coloured images.

For the experienced cake decorator, hand cut stencils are probably the best choice, enabling you to design your own.

MAKING A STENCIL

Select a suitable motif from a book, wrapping paper or greetings card (see note on page 63). Draw the motif or get someone to design something for you. The next stage is to adapt the drawing as a stencil, for this you will need to integrate 'ties' into the motif to keep the stencil together. Ties are the links or solid parts of the design, without these the motif would resemble a silhouette when cut out. Decide where the ties need to be included and draw them in. Ties should only be used where absolutely necessary, keep them to a minimum and try to utilize a part of the design to form a tie, using them cleverly to make them less conspicuous. Use the basic drawing to help determine which parts will make the most effective ties. Clean up and outline the design.

Start with a basic drawing of the motif.

Decide upon the best placing of the ties.

Clean up and outline the design.

Transferring design on to stencil card.

Cutting out stencil with a craft knife.

The completed stencil ready for use.

CUTTING A STENCIL

Make a tracing of the prepared design and transfer it to the parchment paper or stencil card. If using parchment paper, trace the design with a hard 2H pencil, then trace the outline on the reverse of the tracing paper with a softer HB pencil. Place the tracing on the parchment and outline with a 2H pencil. It can sometimes be difficult to see the image on the oiled parchment, and a better definition will be reproduced in this way.

Position the stencil paper or card on a cutting board and cut out using a sharp craft knife. This can be a time consuming process, but it is worthwhile making a neat job of the cutting as an oiled parchment stencil will last a long time if correctly cleaned and stored between use.

Take care when cutting lines that are very close together, apply a firm pressure on the craft knife to ensure good clean cuts. If you do make a mistake and cut out the wrong part, especially if nearing completion of a very intricate stencil, you can repair it by pressing a piece of masking tape on the reverse of the damaged part, then turn the stencil over and re-cut the area. This will not last as long as a perfectly cut stencil, but will save re-cutting a new one.

USING A STENCIL

FLAT STENCILLING ON A CAKE
Place the stencil on the iced surface. Ensure that the stencil cut-outs are in exactly the right position on the cake top or side. With your forefinger and thumb, hold down the stencil firmly on the surface, or secure the stencil with pieces of masking tape as shown. Do not allow the stencil to move during the stencilling operation that follows. For a simple two colour image, such as the dog motif shown, use small pieces of masking tape to mask off the cut-out of the dog.

Using a palette knife, spread a small

To make curved stencilled off-pieces for flower decorations or waterlily centres, dry the shapes on waxed paper resting in half a cardboard tube as shown. New plastic rainwater pipe also makes good formers.

but sufficient amount of suitably coloured icing across the stencil to cover the required cut-out. If you are using your finger and thumb to hold the stencil steady, then spread the icing away from the finger and thumb to prevent the stencil lifting and buckling; this should not occur if using masking tape. Remove the mask from the dog area. If necessary, mask the stencilled collar before repeating the technique with the second colour of icing to complete the head and body of the dog.

Without disturbing the stencil (movement could distort the shapes), start at the unheld end and gently and carefully lift and peel off the stencil. If you have difficulty in starting to lift the stencil, slip a thin palette knife under the corner.

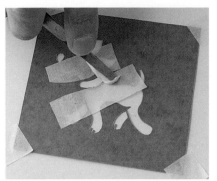

Spreading icing evenly over the stencil.

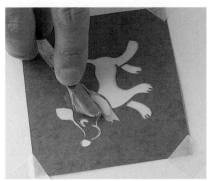

Applying a second colour of icing.

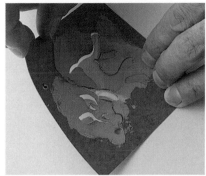

Carefully removing the stencil.

STENCILLED OFF-PIECES

Use exactly the same technique as for flat stencilling, but stencil the required shapes on to strips of waxed paper or plastic film. Hold down the waxed paper or plastic film while removing the stencil after spreading the icing across. If preferred, secure the paper or plastic with small pieces of masking tape to prevent movement during stencilling.

The stencilled off-pieces may be dried flat as for butterfly wings or over a suitable former shape to make curved petals, like the waterlily decoration shown.

CLEANING AND MAINTENANCE

PARCHMENT AND PLASTIC TYPES

After each use, place the stencil in the sink under lukewarm water. Allow the water to flow over the stencil until no traces of icing remain. Remove the stencil from the water and drain. Place the stencil flat on a clean tea-towel and pat dry. Allow the stencil to dry fully for a few hours, then store flat ready for use.

If you intend to store a number of stencils together, interleave them with sheets of smooth paper or thin card.

METAL TYPE

Wash as for parchment stencils, although hot water may be used, which will dissolve the icing or remove the food colour a little quicker. Carefully dry the stencil with a soft cloth or tea-towel. Take care not to damage or snag the intricate parts of the stencil with the cloth when drying. Return them to their original packing.

The stencilled dog motif can be further enhanced as shown by adding extra piping detail for the eye, nose, collar and grass, thus creating a more interesting and colourful decoration for a cake top.

A delicate stencilled waterlily.

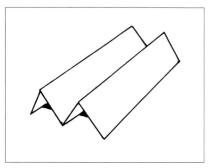

Make a simple 'V' shaped former.

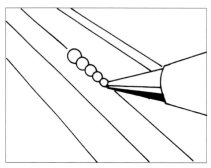

Piping the body shape.

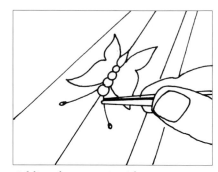

Adding the stamens with tweezers.

BUTTERFLIES

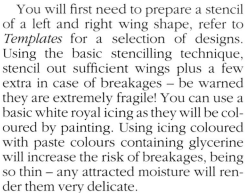

One of the most delicate forms of decoration widely used on celebration cakes, and in particular wedding cakes, is the butterfly. There are various methods that can be employed to produce quite individual variations such as piping, runout, painting and filigree. However, by far the most realistic type is the stencilled variety. The method of stencilling produces a paper-thin wing which can be painted with life-like detail before being assembled into beautiful decorations.

You will first need to prepare a stencil of a left and right wing shape, refer to *Templates* for a selection of designs. Using the basic stencilling technique, stencil out sufficient wings plus a few extra in case of breakages – be warned they are extremely fragile! You can use a basic white royal icing as they will be coloured by painting. Using icing coloured with paste colours containing glycerine will increase the risk of breakages, being so thin – any attracted moisture will render them very delicate.

Allow the wings to dry completely before attempting to paint them. It is a good idea not to remove them from the waxed paper or film until you have painted them. This will enable you to work on and handle them more easily. Refer to *Painting* as a guide to applying food colours to icing, then paint on the wing detail. A few examples of pattern can be seen here but for greater reference borrow a book from the library.

Having prepared and painted the wings, assemble them into butterflies and finish them as shown above. First make a simple 'V' shaped former in which to position the wings whilst they dry. Fold a piece of thick card as shown. Decide upon the wing position you require for the butterflies and close or flatten the 'V' shape accordingly. Use a No. 1 tube (tip) with suitably coloured icing to pipe the body shape. You can pipe a bulb with a tapered body, a tapering rope body or a series of bulbs graduating in size. Carefully remove a matching left and right wing from the waxed paper and position in the former.

While the icing is still soft, insert a coloured fine wire flower stamen into the head using tweezers, these represent the antennae (Note: stamens are NOT EDIBLE). If you prefer to keep your decorations completely edible, pipe two short spikes for antennae using a No. 1 tube. Dry, then finish with a piped bulb on the end.

Stencilled decorations have an appeal all of their own, the flowers are totally different to the piped type and other shapes such as the bells are thinner and more delicate than runouts. Try embellishing the basic flowers, hearts and bells using piped lines, dots, powder colour and gold and silver – the variations are infinite.

HEARTS, BELLS AND FLOWERS

The basic stencilling technique is used for numerous decorations. Stencil hearts and bells flat on to waxed paper or plastic film, then allow to dry. The prepared shapes can then be further decorated and enhanced as shown. Use edible silver or gold food colouring to make the decorations more suitable for anniversary cakes or simply pipe fancy edges and tiny borders using a fine tube (tip).

To save repeating the stencilling technique for each individual petal, stencil in rows of about five or six petals. Allow the shapes to dry, then pipe a bulb of icing on to waxed paper and insert five or six petals, overlapping to create the flower type desired. You can insert the petals with the points facing outwards or with the round edge facing outward. Finish the flowers with a piped centre and tiny piped dots for stamen. When dry, remove from the paper and use as required.

Stencilling on the side of a cake.

Stencilling with several colours of icing.

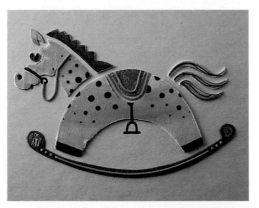

A plain stencil painted with food colour.

A stencil textured with coloured sugar.

STENCILLING ON CAKE SIDES

To stencil on to the curved side of a round cake, simply position the stencil on the cake side and attach with small pieces of masking tape. Alternatively, attach the stencil to a band of paper that can be placed around the cake and secured with masking tape. Before carrying out the stencilling, you may find it easier using a tilter to angle the cake. Apply the icing with the palette knife in a vertically upright position, moving sideways.

MULTI-COLOURED STENCILS

Stencilling in its simplest form is executed using one colour only, providing a quick and easy method of cake decoration – the finished image taking on a somewhat silhouette appearance with only the outline to indicate detail. By introducing one or more colours, the stencil takes on a different effect.

The basic principle of applying the icing is exactly the same as using a single colour, except that cut-out areas of the stencil are blanked out with masking tape until the particular colour for them is applied. Two colour stencilling is described on page 111 for the dog with a coloured collar. The parrot stencil opposite is worked with six different colours of icing, the branch and leaf are painted with food colouring. An alternative method would be to stencil in two colours and paint or pipe on the extra detail as shown for the rocking horse, which was stencilled in grey and brown icing.

TEXTURED STENCILS

Apart from the introduction of extra colour, stencils can also be textured to give a contrast of surfaces. This is particularly useful for animals to depict fur or for trees and foliage on landscapes. Secure the stencil on the cake, stencil the icing and then sprinkle with coloured sugar (see page 81). Remove any excess sugar and peel away the stencil. The dog shown had parts masked out before the textured areas were applied.

STENCILLED CLOWN

The stencilled clown above is shown on a plain royal icing coated board in order to emphasize the effect of stencilling. The design is not restricted to a round cake and would befit a child's birthday cake of any shape. Complete with a suitable piped border, the cake would provide an eyecatching centrepiece for a party table. The painted stencil technique (see page 114) was used for the clown. The figure was stencilled in white icing, allowed to dry and then brightly painted with food colouring. Using this technique enables you to add fine detail that is sometimes difficult to achieve solely with a stencil; such as the holes and cotton on the buttons, the white highlights on the red nose and shoes to make them appear shiny.

Variations on this basic clown figure could be the use of the multi-coloured stencil technique (see page 114) involving the application of coloured icings, and texture introduced in the form of coloured caster (superfine) or granulated sugar (see page 81). Added interest could be provided at the stage of preparing the stencil by cutting a series of circles around the clown's head to appear as balls being juggled. To add this juggling theme after stencilling, simply pipe bulbs of coloured icing directly on to the icing.

AIRBRUSHING

With the increase in new techniques and ideas in royal icing work and sugarcraft and the ability by many cake decorators to combine them creatively, the airbrush has become an invaluable extra item of equipment for achieving spectacular effects with edible colours.

This is not to say that you must purchase an airbrush before you can decorate cakes, far from it. You can still achieve beautiful results using other techniques in the book and just basic tools and equipment. The airbrush is really for the advanced cake decorator.

The airbrush and its components are precision instruments. Before starting to use one, you must understand how it functions, how to maintain it and ensure maximum performance, and also be aware of its full potential.

RETIREMENT COTTAGE CAKE

This most effective border is created off the cake in the form of runout drops of icing piped on to waxed paper and allowed to dry. The drops are then attached to the cake and linework is used to link the design together. The use of the airbrush provides an interesting background for the painted cottage.

THE AIRBRUSH

The airbrush works on the principle of internal atomization. Compressed air flows through a nozzle which supplies liquid food colouring. A partial vacuum at the front of the nozzle aperture makes the food colouring flow. The food colouring is then mixed with the compressed air and atomizes into tiny droplets to form a fine spray. The spray is controlled by a lever which regulates the ratio of air and food colouring. The type of control, which alters the characteristics of the spray, identifies the different sorts of airbrushes available – single-action, double-action and independent double-action – making it a little easier to choose from the vast array of models.

SINGLE ACTION

This type of airbrush has only one control. When the push-button control is operated, the airflow draws the food colour out to produce a spray. Because there is only one control, the ratio of food colouring to air cannot be altered. The only way to create different effects with this type of airbrush is to vary the distance of spray.

DOUBLE-ACTION

Variable colouring flow is made possible by the double-action brushes. The control lever operates the air and food colouring – when the lever is drawn back the flow of both air and colouring increases. The ratio of food colouring to air cannot be varied even with this type of airbrush.

INDEPENDENT DOUBLE-ACTION

This type of airbrush is the most popular and inevitably more expensive. The ratio of food colouring to air is variable and is controlled easily by pressure exerted on the finger lever. Pressing the lever down controls the supply of air and a backward pulling movement allows variable release of food colouring.

To explore the possibilities of this airbrush, a line can be sprayed as narrow as that produced by a fine piping tube (tip) and then continue to spray a large area of even colour in a single spray. If you wish to use airbrushing techniques to the full, this is the airbrush to buy.

DESK CLIP

A simple and inexpensive desk clip can be purchased from your art shop or airbrush supplier. This will enable you to safely leave the airbrush aside when not in use and help prevent spillage. The clip also holds the airbrush firmly upright while you pour in the food colouring ready for use.

Airbrush with compressor and aerosol propellant.

MAINTENANCE

Neglecting the care and maintenance of your airbrush may mean that the upkeep of your equipment in the long term becomes very expensive, due to what could be costly service and repair charges.

It is essential that the airbrush is cleaned after each session of use, otherwise it may become clogged with food colouring and will render the tool useless. Refer to the manufacturer's instruction manual provided with the airbrush, as each make and model of airbrush has to be dismantled in a slightly different way for cleaning.

To ensure true colours and good definition, the airbrush should be flushed through with water after removing any remaining food colouring from the reservoir ready for a change of colour. Apart from regular cleaning of the food colouring channels, you should always check the needle in the nozzle is clean and straight. A sure sign of a bent needle is uneven, spattered colour; if this happens, replace the needle immediately. Never try to insert anything in the nozzle to clear it. Regular servicing by an expert is strongly recommended.

AIR SUPPLIES

If you plan to use the airbrush regularly, it would be wise considering investing in a compressor. Alternatively, for the small user or if you want to save money by experimenting first before buying a compressor, a simple aerosol propellant is the answer.

AEROSOL PROPELLANT
For the beginner, this is usually the first choice. Experience can be gained by using this type of air supply which is quite inexpensive. When you become more interested or practised, the extra cost of more substantial air supply would be well justified.

The advantages of aerosols are their lightness, portability, quietness and the fact that no electrical supply is required to power them.

A disadvantage of this system is that as the air in the can is used up, the pressure falls considerably and will suddenly end completely without much of a warning except for a spattered effect to the spray which could end up on your cake – so be warned! As a precaution to this disadvantage, a metered valve is available, this shows how much air is left in the can.

COMPRESSORS
As with the actual airbrush, there are a wide range of compressors. A basic mini compressor is ideal for royal icing work, having the facility for a single air hose to operate one airbrush which is usually sufficient for the work of a cake decorator. Mini compressors consist of an electric motor driving a tiny piston or diaphragm. They are fairly inexpensive, costing about the same price as a good airbrush. A disadvantage of this type sometimes is that the air comes directly from the compressor and has a tendency to flow in short pulses which can sometimes affect the flow of food colouring. As water filters are not normally fitted to mini compressors, this pulsing effect can lead to tiny droplets of water on your icing surface.

The larger compressors usually incorporate a reservoir which stores air at a constant pressure. Operation is either diaphragm or piston type, each having its own advantages. Because it is oil-free, the diaphragm compressor does not require an oil filter to be attached. Piston units are much sturdier and can be used to generate a higher pressure.

PREPARATION

Before commencing, you will need:

DRAWING EQUIPMENT
For planning your motifs and designs. You may need to enlarge or reduce the size of your design, instructions for this can be found on page 63.

MASKING MATERIALS
These are used to contain the flow of food colourings within a specific area:

Paper and Thin Card
Use this to mask out both large and small areas, or to cut specific shapes.

Plastic Templates
You no doubt will have a selection of various plastic templates in your work box that you use to draw circles, ovals and other shapes. Plastic rulers and bendable French curves are also useful. Acetate plastic available from art shops

can be used to make masks with the added advantage that you can see the work as you progress.

Masking Tape
This is also very useful especially for tiny, intricate areas.

Cotton Wool
You may not always want to produce hard edges of colour, cotton wool used as a mask creates a soft tonal effect when the colour is sprayed adjacent to it – ideal for making clouds or smoke.

Torn Paper
This will produce an effect halfway between using paper with a straight edge or cotton wool, try a combination of both for interesting effects. By holding the torn paper closer or further away from the surface being sprayed you can vary the softness or hardness of the edge.

ERASERS
Pencil erasers and kneadable putty rubbers can be useful both as creative aids and to remove mistakes.

A selection of useful masking materials.

Position of airbrush when spraying.

USING THE AIRBRUSH

TECHNIQUE 1
Hold the airbrush about 6–9 mm (¼–⅜ inch) away from the surface and spray a fine wavy line, stopping the flow of food colouring before cutting off the air supply at the end of each line.

TECHNIQUE 2
Now practise spraying straight thicker strokes by holding the airbrush further away from the surface. You will find that the further the airbrush is from the surface, the thicker the line will be.

TECHNIQUE 3
After trying the exercises described here, hold the airbrush still further away and spray a line, varying the width slightly as you move the airbrush in a wavy fashion.

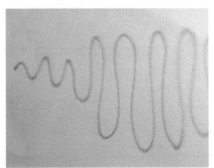

1 Spray close to surface for thin lines.

2 Straight lines of a broader width.

3 A curved line with varying widths.

4 Spraying a script style inscription.

5 Using a straight edge to spray lines.

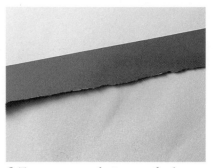

6 Torn paper mask gives a soft edge.

TECHNIQUE 4
Having mastered straight and curved lines, combine the two techniques and try writing your name or a useful inscription in a continuous flowing script style.

TECHNIQUE 5
Using a straight mask of cleanly cut paper or the edge of plastic ruler, spray series of lines keeping the airbrush near the paper edge to produce a dark colour and gradually fade it by slowly lifting the airbrush.

TECHNIQUE 6
To produce a straight line with a slightly softer edge, use a strip of paper torn against the edge of a ruler. Spray against it with a broad even band of colour.

TECHNIQUE 7
The numerous effects that can be produced using paper masks are infinite. The zig-zag angular pattern shown lends itself particularly to the side of a square cake. Pipe lines on the edge of the pattern to emphasize the effect.

TECHNIQUE 8
A curved soft edge can be created by using a piece of paper shaped by tearing rather than cutting. Holding the paper loosely, spray into the torn edge of the

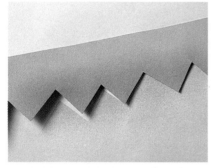

7 A paper cut-out patterned mask.

8 A curved torn paper mask.

9 Circular stencils produce spots.

10 Paper doyleys make lace effect.

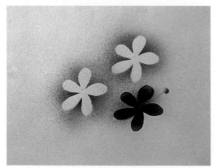

11 Securing with glass headed pins.

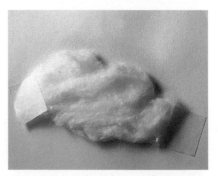

12 Cotton wool produces soft edges.

paper allowing the air to vibrate the paper and produce a soft edge.

TECHNIQUE 9

Based on the technique of stencilling, these spots or balls of colour are sprayed over a piece of card with a cut-out circle removed. Spraying darker on one side of the circle will create a spherical appearance.

TECHNIQUE 10

A paper cut-out such as the pattern of a paper doyley can be used in a similar manner to a stencil by spraying through to create an attractive lace type effect suitable as a decoration for the top or sides of a cake.

TECHNIQUE 11

Small paper masks can be difficult to keep in place as the pressure of the airbrush will blow them away. Here the flower shapes are held securely in position using a glass headed pin which is carefully removed when spraying is complete.

TECHNIQUE 12

Cotton wool makes an excellent mask for producing soft edges and especially outlines for clouds when making landscapes. Pull off random shapes and sizes of cotton wool and hold in place with small pieces of masking tape. Put the tape under the cotton wool if requiring a full outline.

WINDMILL SCENE

Having mastered the holding position of the airbrush and the many spraying and masking techniques that can be used to create individual effects, you will be able to apply a coloured cake side pattern or compose a picture, scene or landscape. To enable you to prepare the necessary drawings, templates and masks to produce a detailed scene, the steps below show how to plan for each stage.

First select a suitable scene and make a drawing of all the necessary detail, the windmill scene can be found in *Templates*. Transfer the drawing on to the cake top and then prepare a card template to use as a mask for the areas you do not require to be sprayed, in the example; the windmill. Secure the mask to the cake surface with masking tape, then position and attach cotton wool for the clouds (Technique 12), and a torn paper mask for the ground level (Technique 8), keep the other half of this mask for later use. Commence by spraying blue colour for the sky, creating a darker colour near the paper ground level mask and fading out the colour towards the top of the windmill. Remove both the cotton wool and paper ground level masks but leave the windmill shape in position. Using the other half of the ground level paper mask, blank out the sky area as shown, then spray the green, brown and orange tones to represent the grass and shrubs. Again spray darker near the mask and fade out the colour gradually towards the base of the scene. All the masks including the windmill can now be removed and the windmill and other detail painted on directly, see *Painting*.

Blue colour sprayed over masks.

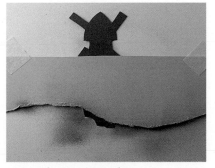

Ground tones sprayed on.

The finished scene.

PAINTING

There will no doubt be times when you need to apply colour directly on to the cake surface or on to a plaque to depict a scene, figure, badge or other detailed motif. Painting on cakes is a most attractive aspect of cake decoration.

Many people are afraid to attempt painting on to a cake or even on to a plaque. The basic techniques already mastered in this book will give you confidence, even though you may never have painted before. Understanding colour, handling paint brushes and brush embroidery are all techniques that will make painting easier.

Try a few of the following basic painting techniques on paper first, then move straight on to a royal icing coated board.

SNOW CAKE WITH SKIER

A cold frosty appearance is emphasized on this cake by the use of cold blue and green colours with the sugar-coated icing to represent snow. The trees are made as runouts and, when dry, fixed into the icing. The shaded sky colour is applied using an airbrush and the skier is directly painted on to the icing surface.

PREPARATION

The following list of equipment will no doubt already be found in your workbox. Assemble everything before starting.

FINE PAINT BRUSHES
Use good quality sable brushes in a range of smaller bristle sizes, you can build up a set as you progress. A few larger hair type brushes are also useful for applying larger areas of colour.

WHITE BASE MEDIUM
This is available in powder and paste form from sugarcraft shops. The powder is first mixed with water to produce a thin creamy consistency. It is used as a base to which colour is added. Using colour for painting without a base will lead to streaky and patchy colour, especially on large areas.

COLOURINGS
You can choose between liquid and paste colours. The paste type ones are usually more concentrated and will not dilute the white base powder too much. With liquid colours you will need more to produce strong shades. The more comprehensive your range of colours is, the less mixing you will need to do.

TRACING PAPER AND SCRIBER
Use tracing paper for transferring the design on to the icing. The scriber is for transferring the design if you prefer the pin-pricking method as opposed to using a pencil.

PALETTE
Either buy an artist's palette (dish type) or use a clean plastic egg tray, or even a dinner plate.

You will also require pencils, for tracing and transferring the design, a water container and absorbent kitchen paper or cloth for wiping and drying brushes.

STARTING TO PAINT

Once you have assembled the equipment and materials needed for painting, find yourself a work surface that will allow you to sit at a comfortable height. Make sure there is enough space to work, a confined area with pots of water and coloured paint is sure to result in spillage!

All the techniques described can be used on runout work or flat coat icing.

TRANSFERRING THE DESIGN
Transfer the selected design on to the plaque or icing coat of the cake ready to start painting. Use one of the methods described on page 64.

Take care to position the design accurately, allowing for other decoration such as lettering. The design can be secured with masking tape while transferring to prevent movement.

MIXING THE COLOUR
Start by using a teaspoon to deposit a small amount of white base powder or

Equipment and materials for painting.

Mixing the white base medium with colour.

paste on to a palette or plate. Using a paint brush, add water to the powder a little at a time and mix until a creamy consistency is achieved. Paste colour will require less water to obtain a similar consistency.

Using the tip of a cocktail stick (toothpick), add small amounts of the desired colour to the mixture, blending in thoroughly until it is evenly mixed. The colour is now ready to apply to the icing surface.

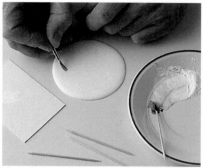

Painting main areas in broad strokes.

Starting shading using darker paint.

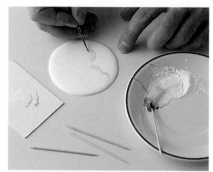

Blending darker and lighter colours.

Increasing the darker area.

Outlining with a paint brush.

Outlining with a sugarcraft pen.

APPLYING COLOUR

Use the brush drier rather than wet. If the brush is overloaded with liquid, the capillary action as you touch the icing will cause the liquid to rush out and soak the icing, dissolving it and leaving a hollow. Take your time, always painting with a dryish brush, rather than trying to hurry the work with a wet brush.

Paint the colour on in broad strokes to cover the main areas. Use smaller strokes and smaller brushes for smaller areas of work.

SHADING

Once the 'flat' colour has been applied, if painted on correctly it will dry quite rapidly and you can continue to work. As a guide to help you, mark a small arrow on your original design, in say the top right hand corner, to indicate the direction of the light source, this will assist greatly in getting the right shading in the right areas.

In this case, the light is coming from the top right. This means that all the shaded or darker areas will fall on the bottom left of each part of the design.

This method works for most illustrations but for some of the more intricate scenes or paintings of buildings, you may need to observe from life or photographs to get more accurate results.

To apply the shading, add some brown or black (even blue depending on the colour) to the colour to be shaded. Brush on a small amount and immediately rinse the brush in water, dab it on a clean cloth or piece of absorbent kitchen paper to take up any excess moisture and leave it just lightly moist. Use the moist brush to blend the dark colour with the lighter colour beneath as shown. Do not over-work the two colours or the effect will be lost, plus the water and movement of the brush will dissolve the icing. The aim of this technique is to remove the 'definite' line where the dark and light colour meets and soften it to produce a shaded effect.

You can darken the colour still further and increase the darkness of the shadow by repeating the above technique.

OUTLINES

Outlines are not always necessary but do tend to give the painting a neat finished look. They also tidy up any uneven edges that you may have made.

USING A PAINT BRUSH
Use a dark colour, such as brown, black or deep blue, and a fine paint brush to carefully follow the outlines visible from the tracing or pin-pricking edges.

USING A SUGARCRAFT PEN
Sugarcraft pens are useful for outlining, again use a dark colour and do not press on too hard. The tips of the pen are quite soft and susceptible to flattening.

HIGHLIGHTS

Having completed painting and outlining you may feel that your image needs highlighting. Highlights are bright spots or lines to indicate light reflection. They certainly add sparkle to a painting, particularly on the dark eyes of painted figures and animals.

To add highlights use a fine brush and just the white base mixture. Make sure the dark colour that you intend to highlight has dried fully otherwise the colours may merge. If the white is not strong enough, allow it to dry, then paint over again with a second application of white.

TEXTURES

Introducing textures into a painting will add more depth and interest.

Simply add a small amount of royal icing to the colour mixture to thicken it slightly. Brush the icing on, leaving the interesting brush strokes quite prominent. You can use straight, curving, swirling or stippling strokes.

Far Left: Highlighting using a brush and white base medium.

Left: This windmill scene uses textures in both light and heavy applications. For the foreground, green, yellow, orange and brown tones have been used.

Designs for these painted plaques are included in Templates.

Sleeping mouse plaque at the completed painting stage, ready for further decoration.

PAINTED PLAQUES

Apart from the obvious use of directly painting a scene or figure on to a cake top or plaque, many interesting pictures can be created by giving a three-dimensional effect to the feature. The plaques shown opposite consist of a basic painted scene and a bird, both enhanced by the use of relief decoration in the form of flowers and foliage. The Christmas plaque has a poinsettia, holly leaves and berries arranged in an attractive flowing curve to frame the painting and create a feeling of depth and distance to the view. The bird plaque features tiny piped blossom flowers attached at natural intervals on the painted branch, again bringing life and interest to the overall image.

The sleeping mouse plaque above illustrates a stage in the creation of these three-dimensional centrepieces. The left-hand side of the painted scene will be further decorated with flowers and leaves piped separately, then attached with icing to the plaque.

MODELLING

To make the various models and ornaments for use on celebration cakes, some of the traditional and modern skills of royal icing work are required. The techniques are used to prepare individual parts which are then assembled into the finished models. Refer to the relevant sections for detailed instructions. Some new techniques and more useful hints are included which will encourage you to create your own original model and ornament designs.

PETAL GAZEBO BRIDE CAKE

This spectacular bride cake is a fine example of royal icing work. The basic petal shape of the cake is reflected in the design of the gazebo ornament. Neatly piped linework is used as a feature decoration on the cake side panels and to follow the shape of the matching top and base collars. Stencilled flowers tucked into the sides add a delicate touch of colour and interest.

21ST ORNAMENT

First make the base of the ornament. Prepare a tracing of the base plinth (see *Templates*) and place a piece of waxed paper over. Using a No. 1 tube (tip), outline the shape and the broderie anglaise detail. Flood-in the shape using prepared run-icing, taking great care to work neatly around the cut-out areas using a fine paint brush. Also make the numerals 21 using the same technique (see page 87). When dry, paint the numerals with silver food colouring using a fine paint brush. Allow to dry.

With all the parts prepared you are ready to finish the ornament. Use a No. 0 tube to pipe the outline detail on the broderie anglaise. With the same tube, pipe a tiny picot dot edging around the outside of the scallop shape. Attach the numerals to the base with a little royal icing and support with small blocks of wood or polystyrene until completely dry. Position and attach the ornament on the cake top and decorate with flowers and ribbons as shown on page 90.

The broderie anglaise patterned base and runout numerals.

The complete 21st ornament.

TULLE FLOWER

Various flowers can be made from this basic technique by using different petal shaped templates and by increasing or decreasing the number of petals within a flower. After selecting the colour of tulle, make a paper or thin card template of the petal shape provided opposite. Fold the tulle to cut out sufficient petals, then place the card template over the tulle and neatly cut around the template and through the layers of tulle.

Place a piece of waxed paper on a cake board, then pin down the tulle shapes using glass headed pins. Pipe around the edge of the shapes using a No. 1 tube (tip) and coloured icing. Allow to dry. When dry, remove the shapes from the waxed paper. Arrange the petals, raising and supporting them off the paper with small pieces of cotton wool. Pipe a large bulb in the centre and insert a few wire stamen with tweezers. The completed flower can be seen on the Frill and Tulle Flower Cake on page 12.

Cutting around template and through layers of tulle.

Stages of piping tulle flower.

PETAL GAZEBO

This delightful cake top ornament combines a number of icing skills that have been described throughout the book. These include runout work, linework piping and filigree. The finished gazebo ornament with its petal shaped base and top is the perfect centrepiece for a petal shaped cake, particularly a wedding cake, but looks equally effective on cakes of other shapes.

PROFESSIONAL TIP
Pipe lace pieces on to waxed paper or plastic film over a template of a suitable shape. Use fresh royal icing and a fine tube (tip). Allow the pieces to dry completely before removing and attaching to the cake with dabs of icing.

1 Outlining the shape with icing.

2 Flooding-in with run-icing.

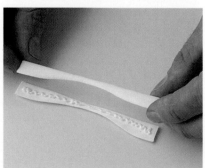

3 Joining supports together in pairs.

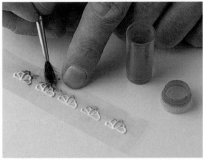

4 Brushing lace pieces with petal dust.   *5 Piping the filigree dome.*   *6 Attaching the roof supports.*

Step 1

Make tracings of two base plinths and one roof and supports from *Templates.* Place a piece of waxed paper over the plinth template and outline using a No. 1 tube (tip).

Step 2

Flood in the outlines neatly with run-icing and set aside in a gentle heat to dry. Continue until all runout sections are completed.

Step 3

Make 12 half section roof supports using the flood-in method above. When dry join together to make six complete supports.

Step 4

Make at least 30 lace pieces using freshly made icing with a No. 0 tube (tip). Pipe the shapes on to waxed paper using the template provided. When dry, lightly colour one half of each shape with petal dusting powder.

Step 5

Cut a 5 cm (2 inch) diameter circle from medium thick card, partly inflate a balloon and push through the hole to make a dome shape. Smear the balloon with a little white fat, then pipe on filigree using a No. 1 tube. Allow to dry. Hold the balloon in front of a gentle heat source, such as the bulb of a reading lamp, and carefully deflate the balloon to release the filigree dome.

Step 6

Attach the small plinth to the top of the large one. Using a No. 0 tube, pipe a tiny picot dot edging around the base of the larger plinth and the curved edges of the roof supports. To enable picot dot edgings to be piped more accurately, position the runout section back over the template design in the book or on your marked tracing. Attach the roof supports to the base with a little icing, supporting until dry.

Attach the roof and dome and decorate with the prepared lace pieces. Pipe a bulb of icing in the centre of the base and insert flower wire. Arrange prepared icing flowers, buds and leaves, and two wired love birds to complete (see opposite).

The flowers are made using the method described in *Stencilling* and shown on page 113. When dry, attach the flowers with icing on to special flower wires to represent stems. The love birds (see page 102) are piped on to wire using a No. 2 tube.

PROFESSIONAL TIP
An alternative to the recommended balloon for the petal gazebo top would be to use a clean, lightly greased table tennis ball.

Arranging the flowers and love birds in the gazebo.

JACK-IN-THE-BOX

Place a piece of waxed paper over the box template in *Templates*. Outline and flood-in using the runout technique. Allow the shapes to dry. Meanwhile prepare the Jack figure using the pressure piping technique on page 107. Mix all the colours of icing required, making them bright and bold for this type of figure. Using tubes (tips) No. 2, 3 and 4, fill the bags and commence piping.

Next paint the box design on the prepared runout pieces, refer to *Painting* for guidelines. You can use the pattern provided or design your own using different colours. Having painted each section, assemble the box, attaching each part together with icing and supporting as shown until dry. Position and attach the box to the cake top and pipe a large bulb of stiff royal icing in the bottom of the box. To stiffen the royal icing, blend in some dry icing (confectioner's) sugar – the icing needs to be firm to support the

PROFESSIONAL TIP
Collect small blocks of wood and polystyrene, also empty tablet bottles, to make excellent supports when assembling models for drying.

figure. Remove the Jack figure from the waxed paper and insert into the icing in the box, supporting until dry. Attach the lid to the box with a little icing and support at an angle with a small block of wood or polystyrene until dry. Conceal the joins of the box with a piped tiny plain shell, using a No. 1 tube.

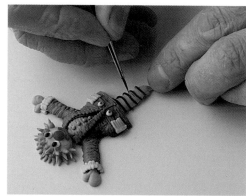

Painting Jack figure.

Painting detail on box side.

Assembling box, attaching with icing.

MOTOR CAR WITH TEDDY

Prepare the shapes required for the car. Trace the outlines from *Templates*. Place a piece of waxed paper over, then outline and flood-in using the runout technique. Allow the shapes to dry. Using food colourings and a fine paint brush, apply the details to each section of the car. Paint the door, wheels, number plate, seat and steering wheel. Assemble the parts together, attaching with icing and supporting until dry. Pipe lines of icing for the bumpers using a No. 3 tube (tip). When dry, paint with gold or silver food colouring. Prepare the teddy using the method on page 104 in *Pressure Piping*. Sit teddy in the car on a bulb of icing.

Painting the dry runout shapes.

Painting detail on the car.

Sitting teddy in the car.

FINISHING TOUCHES

Having spent much time and patience to produce an edible work of art for a special occasion, you will no doubt wish to complement the artistic aspect of the cake itself with attractive trimmings. These finishing touches can personalize the cake or give it your own distinctive mark.

PROFESSIONAL TIP
Alternatives to the traditional cake pillar used to support the cake are the now popular stainless steel spiral cake stands and perspex (plexiglass) supports which eliminate the need for pillars.

COLOUR MATCHING

For most cakes, colour plays a vital role in the initial design planning. It may be that one of the traditional colours associated with boy and girl is selected such as blue or pink. If the cake is for an anniversary, for example choose blue or silver for a silver wedding, red for ruby and peach, apricot or orange to harmonize with gold for a golden wedding.

The obvious and probably the most frequent use of colour matching in royal icing work is in wedding cake design. Often the bride likes any touches of colour or embellishments or even the complete cake to be the same tint or shade as the bridesmaid's dress or flowers. The best way to do this is to request a small swatch of material from the bride.

Colour matching may also be required for celebration cakes made for anniversaries, centenaries or special presentations for clubs, groups and organizations. To carry a theme through the decoration of the cake, ice it in the 'house' or company colour scheme along with the badge, crest or logo. For this type of colour matching, ask for a printed letterhead featuring the colours, or loan a badge, sticker or product displaying the necessary details you require.

To produce the required colour may involve a little experimental work, unless of course you are lucky and the colour is available 'off-the-shelf'.

Colour swatches of material provide a useful reference when designing a wedding cake and in particular colouring the icing and selecting ribbon and trimmings.

COLOUR MIXING

If you are unable to locate the exact colour required, take a small amount of icing in a bowl and a range of similar colours needed to obtain the colour. For instance, for a biscuit colour, you will need orange (tangerine), egg yellow and a couple of shades of brown, such as dark brown and chestnut, to begin with. Use a cocktail stick (toothpick) for paste colour and a dropper for liquid colour. Add small dabs or drops of colour to the icing and mix in thoroughly. After each addition, take out some icing on the tip of the spatula and hold it next to your colour swatch because colour matching while the icing is in the bowl can be somewhat deceiving. Determine if the icing needs more of one particular colour, more of each or if it is too dark add more white icing. Keep mixing and matching until the correct colour is achieved. The colour chart on pages 18 and 19 will help you decide which colours to use when mixing.

RECORDING COLOUR COMBINATION

The above method is fine for a small, one-off amount of a particular colour. For larger quantities, such as the amount required to fully ice and decorate a multi-tiered cake, you will need to record the colour combination. For this you need to weigh an amount of icing and make a note on paper. As you add the colour make a note of the number of drops, in this way you will produce a sort of recipe or formula; it may be something like:

450 g (1 lb) royal icing
2 drops egg yellow colour
1 drop chestnut brown colour
3 drops tangerine colour

For paste colour, I usually make a compound or mixture of the various paste colours used to make a particular

PROFESSIONAL TIP
To further enhance wedding and celebration cakes, they can be displayed on one of the many attractive cake stands now available which give weight and added height to the cake. They can be purchased or hired for the occasion and come in round and square, silver, gold and white.

PINK MARBLE AND ROSE CAKE

Royal iced cakes are normally renowned for the smooth coating that can be achieved; however, this cake breaks a few rules and adds a new dimension in the form of painted colour to create a marbled effect (see page 137). Matching pillars are used and the whole creation is set off with fabric roses and foliage.

special colour and store them in an empty paste colour jar. A miniature measuring spoon provides sufficient accuracy to add the required amount to the icing. One colour I always keep to hand is my own formula for leaf green – far better than the commercial ones.

Recording colour combinations allows you to experiment with the desired colour using only a small amount of icing – the quantities can then be multiplied to make larger amounts. The most beneficial aspect of recording the colour is for future reference, imagine running short of a special colour of icing and being unable to match it perfectly.

CAKE SUPPORTS

The icing boom over the past few years has provided considerable changes in the type and style of stands and pillars used to support multi-tiered cakes. The tubular stainless steel stand is manufactured in numerous curved and multi-curved combinations (see Orange Rose Wedding Cake on page 22).

Cake pillars can now be purchased in a greater choice of heights, shapes and materials, such as gold and silver metallic, white, ivory and cream coloured plastic and even clear perspex (plexiglass). These look stunning on a cake of contemporary design. The traditional plaster pillar, however, is still favourite.

PROFESSIONAL TIP
Tiered cakes can easily be spoiled by incorrectly positioned supports. Take time to make a template for each cake that spaces the pillars out evenly to balance the tiers. Start with deep pillars on the base tier and use slightly shorter ones on the middle tier which support the top tier.

DESIGNER CAKE PILLARS

As discussed, coordinating colour in a design makes a wedding cake appear more finished and complete, in tune with the overall theme of the wedding. So why not take this a stage further and colour the cake pillars to match.

COLOURED CAKE PILLARS

Simply paint the pillars with a non-toxic paint such as poster paint, mixed to the desired tint or shade. The pillars will probably need two coats of paint to give a good finish.

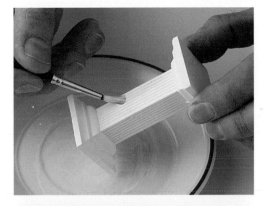

MARBLED CAKE PILLARS

First paint these as for coloured cake pillars, then paint on the marble veining, using a fine paint brush and a darker shade of the base colour used. Paint the marbling on while the base coat is still wet to let the colours merge and create a better effect.

FLORAL CAKE PILLARS

Use plain white pillars (unpainted) or lightly tinted ones. Prepare small piped or stencilled flowers and leaves (see page 113), tinting them with edible petal dusting powder. Mark the stem arrangement on the pillar with a pencil. Pipe the stem with green royal icing using a No. 1 tube (tip), then attractively attach the flowers and leaves. As an extra feature, attach a small stencilled and painted butterfly to one pillar in a group.

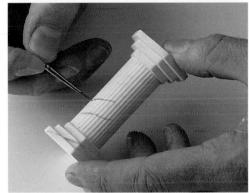

TEXTURED CAKE PILLARS

Prepare some royal icing of the desired colour tint, or use white, then soften the icing slightly with a few drops of cold water. Using a small piece of sponge, apply the prepared icing using a dabbing action to leave an even texture all over the pillar.

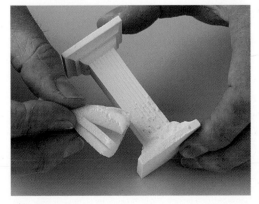

DESIGNER CAKE BOARDS

As with all the other aspects of icing materials and equipment, there is now available an even greater range of shaped cake boards in various sizes. The conventional round and square shapes are still the most popular, but these have now been joined by petal, diamond, oblong, triangular, oval and of course heart, octagonal and hexagonal.

However, if you require other special shapes that are unavailable commercially, you can cut your own. Use a jigsaw and a pattern to cut from 1.5 cm (½ inch) thick wood or wood veneered chipboard. Use a non-toxic adhesive to stick gold or silver board covering paper to the board. The edges can be trimmed with gold or silver band or ribbon.

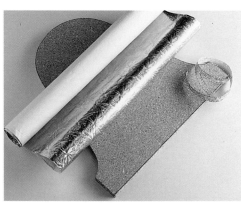

Right: Various cake board shapes.

Far Right: Materials for a special shaped board.

CAKE BOARD DECORATION

PROFESSIONAL TIP
Neatly tied ribbon bows can be added to cakes to give extra decoration. Positioned on the side, top or around the base, providing they are tastefully used they add colour, texture and form. Make your own or buy them ready tied.

Cake boards do look quite attractive as they are, with the gold or silver face exposed around the edge. However, many cake designs do benefit from the addition of ribbon around the board edge. Satin and velvet ribbon looks nice to complement or contrast the colour scheme. Patterned ribbon is also quite useful.

For wedding cakes, try to match the ribbon colour with the colour of the bridesmaid's dress or flowers.

ATTACHING RIBBON

To attach ribbon to the board edge, apply some adhesive to the board and start at the back of the cake so that the join is out of sight. Use a glass headed pin to hold the ribbon and continue pressing it in place until the ribbon meets. Cut off and trim the edge, secure with a pin until the adhesive has set, then remove the pins. Do not use icing to stick the ribbon on to the board, the wet icing sometimes soaks through and stains the ribbon.

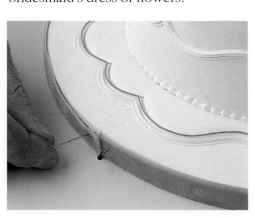

Right: Attaching ribbon to cake board edge.

Far Right: Patterned ribbon makes an attractive edging.

1 *Marking shape of wedge.*

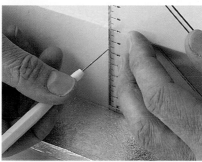

2 *Marking lines on side of cake.*

3 *Cutting just through lines and icing.*

4 *Removing cut wedge.*

5 *Covering cake with waxed paper.*

6 *Tying and cutting ends of bow.*

CUTTING A WEDGE

This finishing touch to a wedding cake adds an extra dimension to the decoration. More importantly it enables the cake cutting part of the wedding ceremony to be executed more graciously than having to cut the cake for real. All the bride has to do is break the decoration with the wedding cake knife and pull the bow to remove a perfectly cut wedge of cake.

Step 1
First mark the shape of the wedge on the cake top of the bottom tier cake. The size is up to you but do not make the wedge too sharp, otherwise handling the point becomes difficult. Use a scriber.

Step 2
Using the scriber again, mark the vertical lines on the cake side with the aid of a small set square.

Step 3
Cut through the lines and just through the royal icing using a thick bladed saw knife or strong craft knife. This wide cut makes it easier for the bride to insert the knife without distorting the coating.

Step 4
Using a clean knife with a wet blade, cut through the marzipan and down to the cake board with a slight sawing action. Wipe the blade clean between cuts to avoid crumbs discolouring the icing.

Step 5
Remove the wedge, then cover the exposed fruit cake and marzipan on the faces of the wedge with waxed paper.

Step 6
Cut enough ribbon to fit around the wedge and make a bow. Trim the tails of the ribbon, then push the wedge back into place. Continue to decorate.

Step 7
The gaps of the cuts will not be very wide, the edges can be piped with a tiny pearl or some linework.

7 *Replacing the decorated wedge.*

EXHIBITION WORK

If you have followed the instructions and advice given throughout the book, you will already be aiming at and achieving high standards of work. High standards do not come easy, they require lots of practise, perseverance and experience. This book will help you a great deal, but you need to be constantly aware of new techniques and new equipment, all of which can be gleaned from sugarcraft exhibitions.

Visiting exhibitions is a most pleasurable experience, meeting other cake decorators, seeing new equipment and more importantly witnessing actual cakes decorated by other decorators, tutors and

PROFESSIONAL TIP
The majority of the templates are actual size for the cakes indicated. However, should you need to reduce or enlarge them to fit cakes of other sizes, simply refer to page 63. You can trace or copy the designs directly from the page ready for use, you may even (for your own personal use only) prefer to photocopy them.

PINK RABBIT CAKE

This typical exhibition style cake is tastefully decorated with matching top and base collars, with side linework following a similar design to that of the collar shape.

The flowers are pressure piped and the centrepiece rabbit motifs are runout (see page 99). Further details for this attractive cake appear on page 146.

authors. To see the beautiful work close-up can help to explain many of your queries regarding various aspects of decoration. Contact the secretary of your local Cake Decorating Club or a branch of The British Sugarcraft Guild, who will advise you how to join and benefit from their local and national shows and exhibitions. The British Sugarcraft Guild also offers a quarterly magazine as part of its membership package.

The majority of people decorate cakes as a hobby, seriously or just a one-off special occasion cake for the family. Others take their hobby or career a stage further and show their work at an exhibition either as a display piece, part of a group project or in a competitive class in a competition. If you slot into the last category and your interest now lies with improving your work even further to prepare for entry in a local or national competition, then the advice, hints and tips that follow will prove most beneficial to your work.

Most competitions offer classes in many if not all the various aspects of sugarcraft, from chocolate work to flower modelling and sugarpaste to gâteaux. In this section much of the information relates mainly, but not exclusively, to royal icing.

THE FIRST STEPS

You will first need to find out where and when sugarcraft exhibitions are taking place, this information you will need well in advance to enable you to plan and prepare your entry. If you join an organization that offers a journal or magazine, you will be constantly kept updated of forthcoming events.

THE SCHEDULE
On finding out about an exhibition that you feel you would like to enter, send immediately for a copy of the Competition Schedule. Remember, before you send for the schedule make sure that you will be able to travel to the venue with your exhibit or that a friend or member of a local group that is entering will take (and exhibit) your work for you.

ENTRY APPLICATION
On receiving and reading your schedule, check that you are eligible to enter the class you wish to exhibit in. It may be a novice or open class, or it may be that you need to be a member of a particular body or organization. It is important to read the rules very carefully. Be aware of what the class is requesting in terms of maximum or minimum size allowed, cost, presentation and the accepted or non-accepted use of edible or non-edible/artificial decorations, and manufactured cake supports. Bear in mind that breaking the rules could mean that your exhibit is disqualified.

REAL CAKE OR CAKE DUMMY
On reading the class requirements, make a note of whether you are asked to decorate a real fruit cake or if you are allowed to use polystyrene or wooden cake dummies. If you do use a dummy, buy the highest quality one you can afford. A smooth unblemished surface to start with will make coating and covering much easier. If the specification requires that you use a real cake for your exhibit, do ensure that you achieve a good coating of marzipan on which to work.

DESIGNING THE CAKE OR PLAQUE

Try to be as original as possible with your cake design, do something to attract the eye of the judges, without being over-adventurous beyond your level of skill. It is better to produce clean neat work of a standard that you can comfortably attain, than to try emulate someone else's work beyond your capabilities.

If you intend to use any templates for off-pieces, for example runout collars, it is better to measure your cake after the final coat then design the collar to fit.

COMPETITION QUALITY ROYAL ICING

The following tips should assist you in producing excellent quality royal icing to obtain high standards of workmanship:
● Use a Bridal Quality extra fine icing (confectioner's) sugar available from specialist suppliers.
● Do not hesitate, even though it is lump free, to sieve the icing sugar three times.

● Use a good quality albumen powder and strain the mixed solution through clean, extra fine muslin (cheesecloth) to ensure the mixture contains no impurities.
● Use the colour matching method described on page 135 to ensure a perfect match to all your work.

CAKE AND BOARD COATING

To achieve as near a perfect cake coating as possible and to make the overall working on and assembly of the complete exhibit easier and more accurate, coat the cake and board separately, as in *Coating Techniques*, with some adjustments.

CAKE SIDE COATING

You may be happy with and achieve sufficiently suitable results using the conventional side coating technique (see page 31) – just remember to take extra care and to keep the board and cake edges free from excess icing. However, do not coat the cake board with the cake in place, do this separately.

Here is an alternative and much used side coating technique among competitive cake decorators:

Step 1
You are aiming to produce a side coating that is perfectly vertical, straight and with no 'rim' of icing at the top edge or more usually at the base. To do this, position the cake as shown, on a cake board or disc of wood cut to a slightly narrower diameter than the cake, all of which should be on a board about 7.5 cm

(3 inches) larger than the diameter of the cake.

Step 2
Using a good strong straight side scraper without any flaws or defects in the coating edge, coat the cake in the conventional manner. A real cake should be sufficiently heavy to keep still, but a light polystyrene dummy will need a weight on top to keep it steady. Do not forget to put a clean piece of greaseproof (waxed) paper between the icing and the weight – you do not want any marks left.

Step 3
Having coated the cake, remove the excess icing as described on page 32, trim off the excess icing around the base using the same technique, but going under the cake or dummy with the palette knife. Leave to dry.

1 Raising cake dummy on a board.

2 Smoothing icing with a side scraper.

3 Removing excess icing from base.

CAKE TOP COATING

Use the same technique for coating the top of the cake as described in *Coating Techniques*, taking even more care with each stage and paying attention to clean and tidy edges.

If using a polystyrene dummy, it will need to be secured so that it does not move while drawing the straight edge across. An easy, quick and reliable solution is to use a cake board with a number of 7.5 cm (3 inch) nails pushed through from the base of the board. Place the dummy on the nails and push down to secure into place. Double-sided adhesive tape is another excellent way to attach dummies to cake boards.

ICING CONSISTENCY
For all the coating techniques remember to adjust the consistency of royal icing for each subsequent coat, the final coat being the thinnest and finest coat.

TAKE-OFF MARKS

If the cake is not being eaten, then it is quite acceptable to use very fine sandpaper to remove small blemishes and take-off marks, which incidentally at this level of work should be a minimum. The use of softer royal icing and more pressure (with the side scraper) on each subsequent coat of icing means that very little icing stays on the cake, the majority of the final coat should be taken off with the scraper, the icing being 'forced' into the coat beneath to form an extremely smooth surface. Using this technique should result in little or no take-off mark being visible. Many competitive cake decorators put quite a heavy weight on the top of the cake (without cracking the surface) so that they can really press hard on the side with the scraper to produce this perfect coat.

This same principle applies to the top of the cake – softer icing, more pressure on the straight edge resulting in a thinner coat.

COATING THE CAKE BOARD

Again to accomplish excellence in your work, the board needs to be perfectly flat ready to accept the coated cake. This can be achieved in two ways.

Coat the board, treating it as the top of the cake, using a straight edge to smooth it off. Complete three or four coats.

Alternatively, place a weight on the centre of the board and using a palette knife to apply icing, rotate the board with the other hand and coat in one complete circular movement. Repeat three or four times. For this method you need only produce a perfect band around the edge that will be visible.

The cake board edge must be cleaned between each coat, using a clean, damp cloth.

Coating a cake board with icing.

Coating the outer edge of a cake board.

Cleaning icing from the board edge.

A homemade wooden side piping jig.

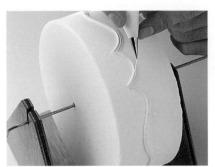

Piping linework on side of dummy.

Plugging hole in dummy with icing.

PIPING ON THE CAKE SIDE

The method described on page 45, using a cake tilter, is most suitable and will produce excellent results. However, if you are working on polystyrene cake dummies and want to pipe shaped panels, you can fit the coated dummy into a specially made jig. This enables you to pipe with the side perfectly horizontal, with the added facility of being able to rotate the cake as you pipe each panel.

You can buy a jig which sandwiches and holds the coated cake between two foam-lined adjustable discs.

You can quite easily make a less sophisticated jig yourself. It requires pushing a metal rod or wooden dowel through the centre of the cake, which in turn rests in the V grooves. Prevent the dummy rotating by securing the rod with a little plasticine.

When the side work is complete, the cake is removed and the hole in the top plugged with matching royal icing. The centre decoration, a painted design or runout figure will neatly cover the slight mark left.

TECHNIQUE TIPS

● Common sense – but do remember, clean hands all the time. Use disposable plastic gloves if you have to pick up the cake or dummy.
● Never talk over a cake or runout collar, the fine spray of moisture from your mouth could spot your cake and spoil it.
● Make lots of spare collars, flowers and motifs, select the best for the cake and keep the others in case of last minute breakages or mistakes.
● Try to cover any take-off mark (which should be minimal at this level of skill) with a linework panel or other side decoration.
● Use fine tubes (tips) when outlining runout pieces or collars to give a high degree of delicacy to your work.
● Ensure a good sheen on runout work by correct drying near a gentle heat source, immediately after flooding-in (see page 93).

● Having attached a runout collar to the top of the cake, it is a good idea to fill the space between the cake and collar with icing. Use a small plastic scraper and then pipe a tiny pearl or shell to make a neat finish.
● Piping extra fine filigree on the reverse side of the runout collar (before attaching to the cake) provides a pleasant surprise for the judge on looking up from the base of the cake – the ultimate detail!
● Use templates for every aspect of the decoration, such as linework, collars, lettering, to ensure as near perfection as possible.
● Any repeated sequences, such as dot formations in runout collar, cut-outs or scratched lines should be consistent, with the same number of dots in each. If it gets to the nitty gritty on a joint first award, you may just win by your attention to detail.

Placing the cake over the base collar.

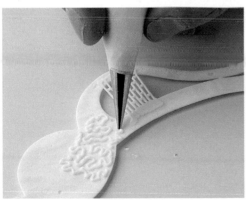

Left: Filling the collar to cake join with icing.

Far Left: Piping filigree on the collar underside.

• Linework is an important part of the finish of your cake and can mean a considerable amount of points towards your final result. Use No. 1, 0 and 00 tubes (tips).

• If you are doing lots of continuous piping, be sure to change the piping bag and refill with fresh icing. The warmth of your hands has a shortening and drying effect on the icing in the bag and will make the task much more difficult with inferior results.

• Ensure really good joins are made when piping linework. Use a fine moist paint brush to bond joins together.

• Keep a check on the distance in between lines when piping parallel. Remember the guide on page 43, the space between should equal the width of the tube (tip) in use.

• For curved linework, use a very slightly softened icing to give you more manoeuvrability.

• Linework sequences should be based on a minimum of three sets of lines and probably up to five sets.

Filling and smoothing join with icing.

Piping a small shell to conceal the join.

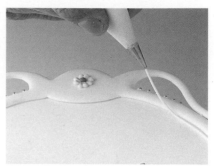
Piping linework around collar edge.

Concealing join with icing beads.

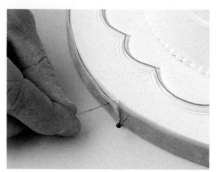
Attaching ribbon to cake board edge.

Attaching staging ticket to the board.

ASSEMBLING A TYPICAL CAKE

Attach the base collar to the board and pipe the linework.

It is easier to work on the cake top decoration while the cake is off the board.

Pipe large bulbs of icing in the centre of the board and accurately position the cake on top, apply a gentle pressure until the cake sits comfortably and level to the collar.

Fill the join and smooth flat with a small plastic scraper.

Pipe a pearl or shell border around the base of the cake to conceal the join.

Attach the top collar and finish as shown.

To finish the cake, pipe the linework on the cake top.

To reduce the risk of breaking the collar while working on the cake top, you may prefer to place the collar on the cake (not attaching it) and pipe one line. Then remove the collar, making a note of its position to the linework. Complete the linework piping, then replace the collar, this time attaching with royal icing.

PACKING AND EXHIBITING

Having completed your cake, attach your staging tickets to the cake board (unless stated differently in the Competition Schedule) with a little glue; do this neatly and keep the labels straight and clean.

Place the cake carefully into a good strong box with a secure lid. Many serious exhibitors have wooden carrying boxes made with a foam covered sliding base section to make positioning and securing in the box easier and much less prone to breakages and damage. These boxes should have a strong handle with which to carry them. Another tip is to tape a small sachet of silica gel crystals (available from chemists) to the inside of the box, this will attract any moisture or dampness, which could soften runout collars, linework or cause colours to run and stain. This is particularly advisable if you are making a long journey with the cake – who knows what the weather conditions will be like!

Label your exhibit box, especially if you have more than one, making staging (displaying) easier on arrival at the competition venue.

Well before leaving for the venue, check that you have the schedule for reference, and a note book to make notes of judges' comments given for your work so that you can utilize the information for future use and therefore improve your standard. Also make sure you have your Competitor Entry Tickets.

On arrival at the venue, to prevent any damage, do not remove the cake from the box until you have found out exactly where to place your exhibit. Then stage your cake in its allocated space, being careful not to damage or move other exhibits that may already be on the table in the near vicinity. Place the cake in the correct viewing position, so that the judges' first look is the one you want them to see.

PROFESSIONAL TIP
To keep the cakes steady in their boxes during transporting, position small blocks of polystyrene up to the board edge – they can be secured to the box base with double sided tape.

WHAT THE JUDGES LOOK FOR

- Does your exhibit comply with the schedule?
- Overall proportion and general appearance – proportion of cake in relationship to its board. Is the appearance pleasing?
- Is the runout collar (if used) in proportion to the rest of the cake?
- If the cake is a multi-tiered cake, are the tiers proportionally balanced to create a pleasing visual appeal?
- Is the design an original or a copied familiar design. Has the competitor created his/her own design?
- Good coating of the top and sides of the cake and board, or just the top in the case of a plaque. Evenness of coating, no air bubbles or take-off marks.
- Is the runout work of a uniform thickness, with good smooth surface and high sheen?
- Border piping should be neat, accurately piped and spaced with an even size to each scroll, shell or bulb.
- Linework piping should have a smooth flowing appearance with neat joins, accurate spacing and overpiping.
- Lace pieces should be fine, neat, accurate, consistent in size.
- Marks (points) will be awarded for visual appeal; proportion; colour; balance; originality; creativity; quality of coating; piping; runouts; linework and of course the feature decoration.
- In the case of real fruit cakes, the judges will cut and taste the cake.

AFTER THE JUDGING

After judging, whether or not you are a winner, try to locate the judges of your cake and discuss the exhibit with them. By talking to the judges you can make notes about aspects of your cake that could be improved upon. Do not be discouraged by the fact you did not win anything for your first entry, or even subsequent entries. Keep trying, use your experiences and put the judges' comments to good use to improve your knowledge and ability.

TEMPLATES

PAGE 69

PAGE 69

PAGE 69

PAGE 66

PAGE 40

PAGE 40

PAGE 69-70

PAGE 82

PAGE 67

PAGE 133

PAGE 67

PAGE 132

PAGE 46

With Love

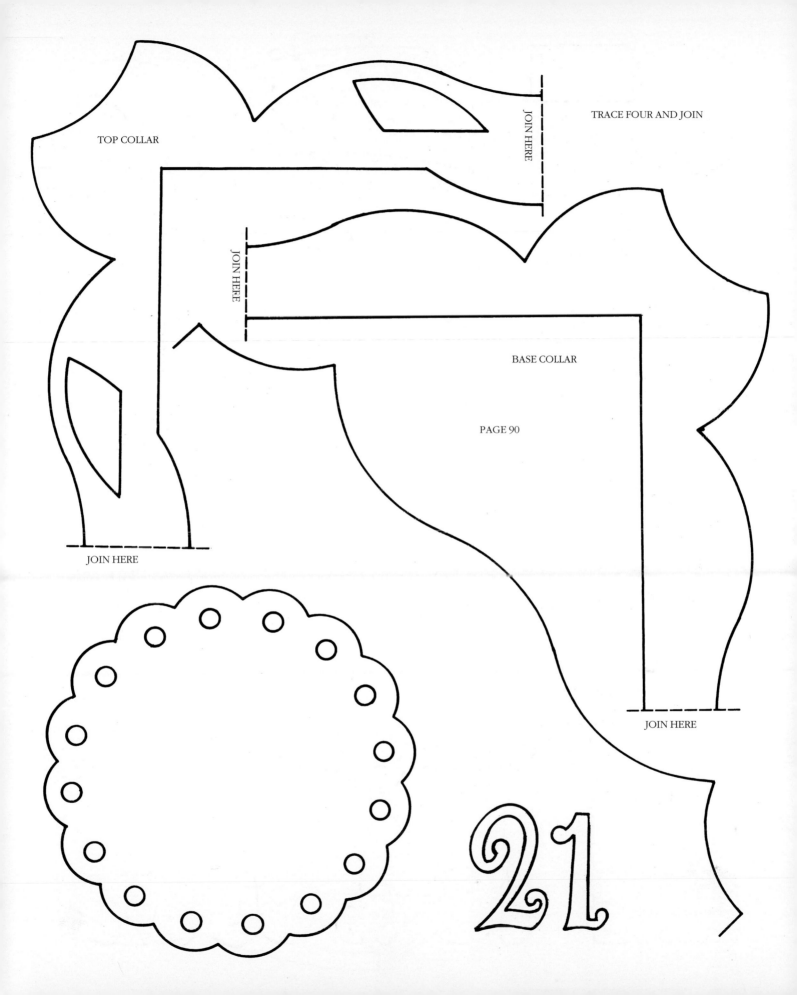

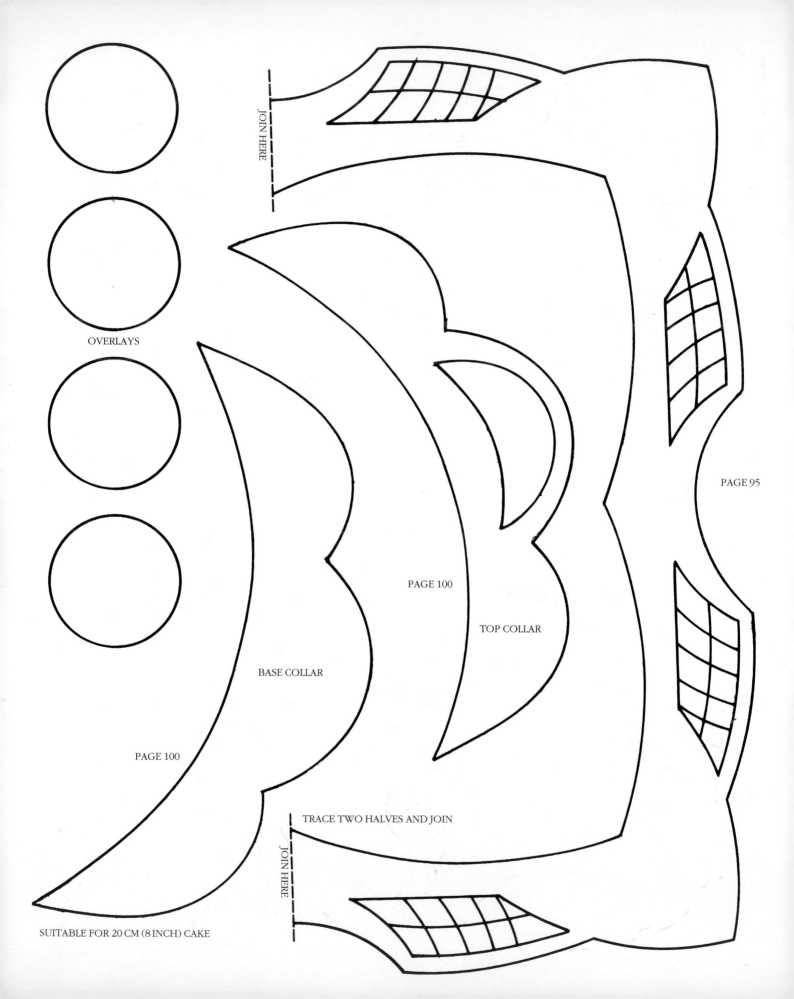

OVERLAYS

JOIN HERE

PAGE 95

PAGE 100

TOP COLLAR

BASE COLLAR

PAGE 100

TRACE TWO HALVES AND JOIN

JOIN HERE

SUITABLE FOR 20 CM (8 INCH) CAKE

PAGE 108

PAGE 108

PAGE 111

PAGE 115

PAGE 114

PAGE 114

PAGE 114

PAGE 116

PAGE 125

PAGE 127

PAGE 55/124

PAGE 126

PAGE 126

PAGE 122

PAGE 122

PAGE 112

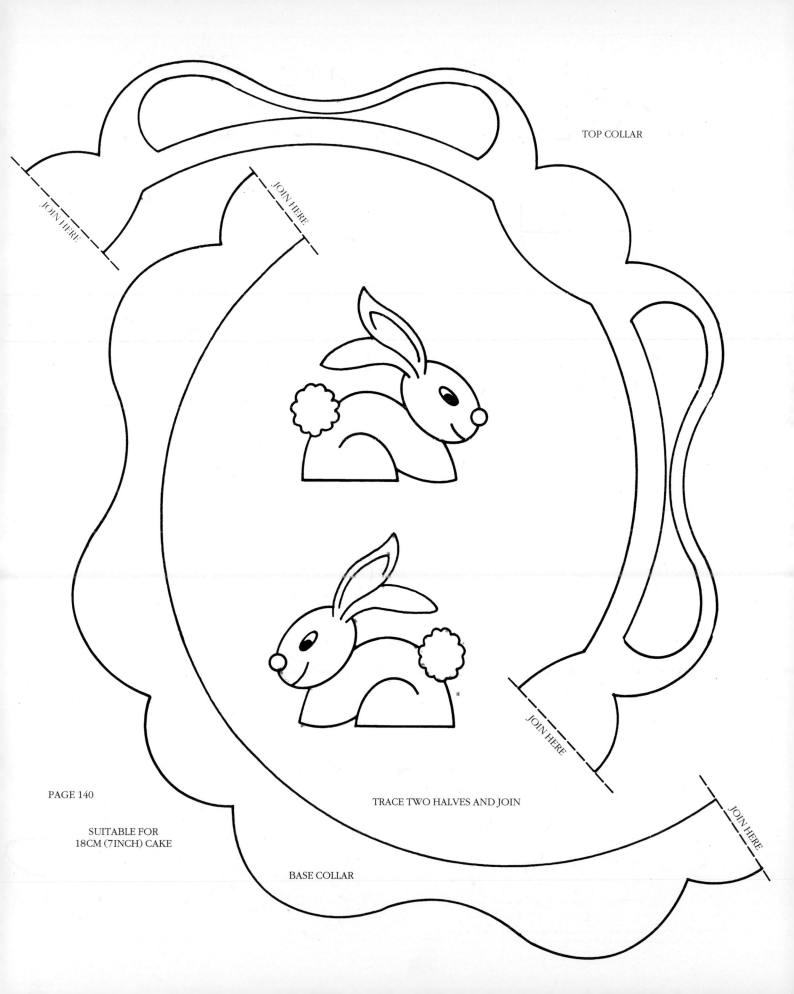

TOP COLLAR

JOIN HERE

JOIN HERE

JOIN HERE

JOIN HERE

PAGE 140

TRACE TWO HALVES AND JOIN

SUITABLE FOR
18CM (7INCH) CAKE

BASE COLLAR

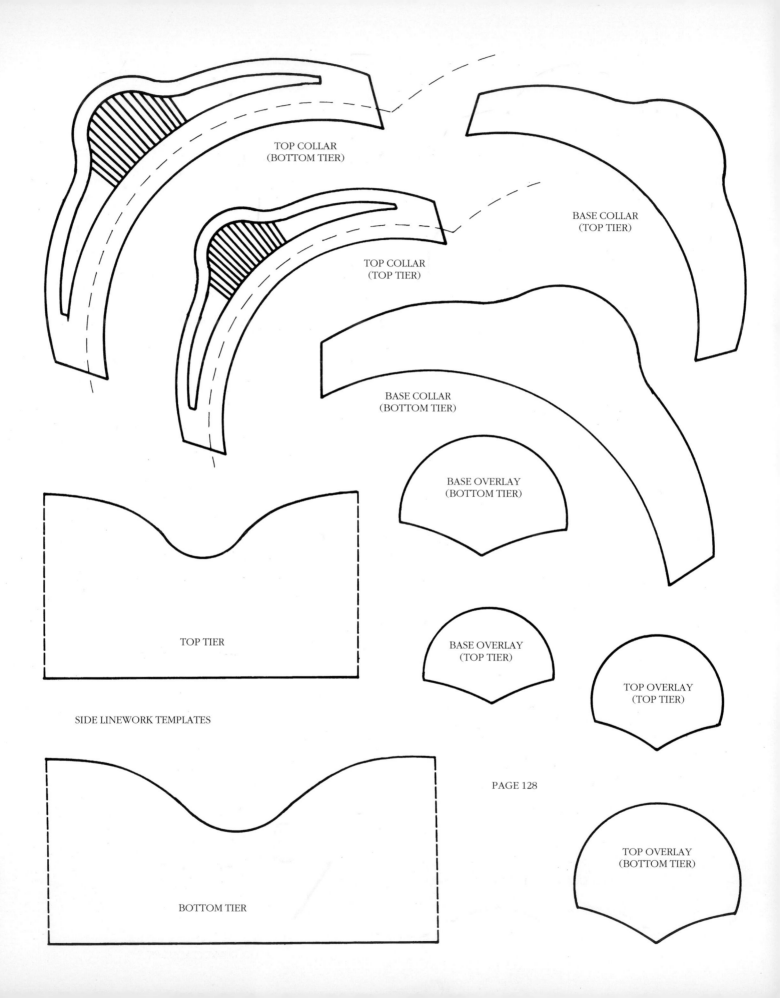

TOP COLLAR
(BOTTOM TIER)

TOP COLLAR
(TOP TIER)

BASE COLLAR
(TOP TIER)

BASE COLLAR
(BOTTOM TIER)

BASE OVERLAY
(BOTTOM TIER)

TOP TIER

BASE OVERLAY
(TOP TIER)

TOP OVERLAY
(TOP TIER)

SIDE LINEWORK TEMPLATES

PAGE 128

BOTTOM TIER

TOP OVERLAY
(BOTTOM TIER)

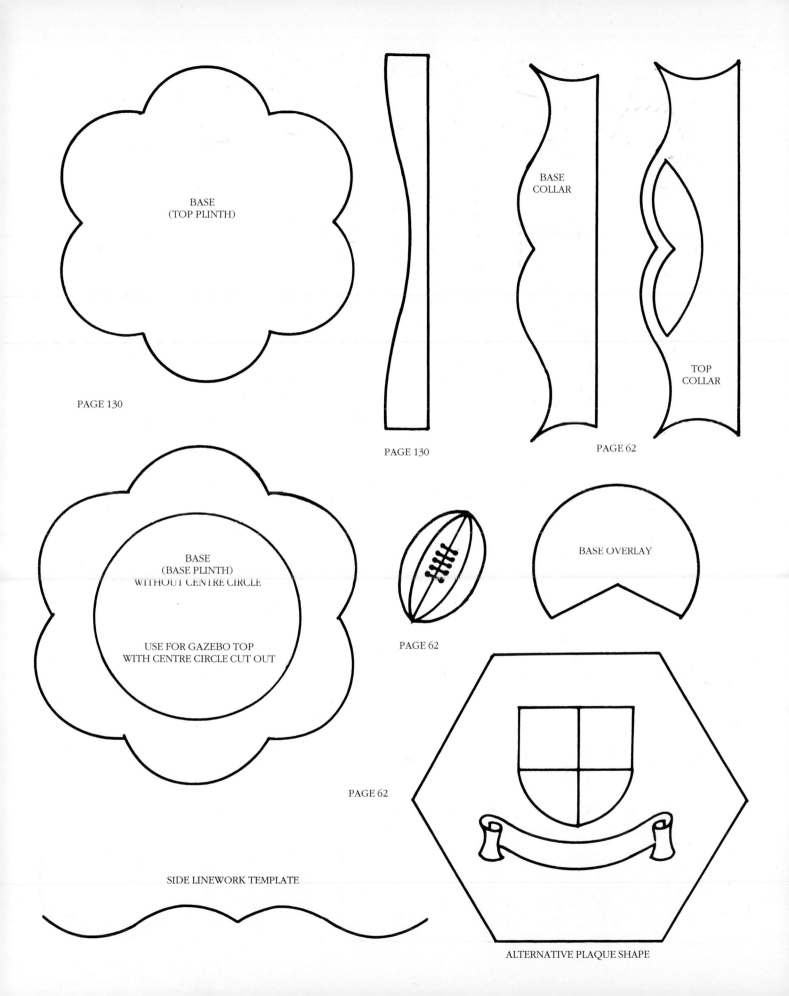

BASE
(TOP PLINTH)

PAGE 130

BASE
COLLAR

TOP
COLLAR

PAGE 130

PAGE 62

BASE
(BASE PLINTH)
WITHOUT CENTRE CIRCLE

USE FOR GAZEBO TOP
WITH CENTRE CIRCLE CUT OUT

BASE OVERLAY

PAGE 62

PAGE 62

SIDE LINEWORK TEMPLATE

ALTERNATIVE PLAQUE SHAPE

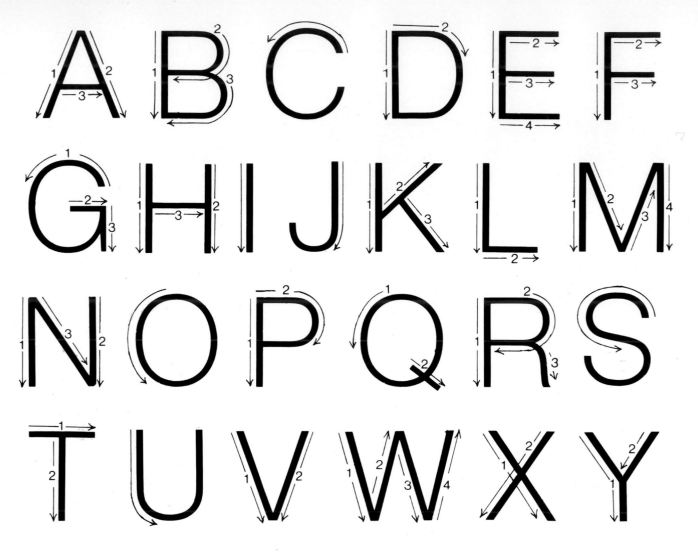

USE THIS ALPHABET OF SIMPLE STYLE LETTERING AS A
GUIDE WHEN PIPING LETTERS TO FORM WORDS OR NAMES.
THE NUMBERS ADVISE IN WHICH ORDER TO PIPE
WITH THE ARROWS ILLUSTRATING WHICH DIRECTION.
REFER TO THE SECTION *LETTERING* FOR MORE INFORMATION.

INDEX

aerosol propellant 118
Airbrushing 116–121:
    maintenance 117
    techniques for using 119
air supplies 118
albumen:
    pure hen 13
    substitutes 14
apricot glaze 25, 26

basket weave 72
bells 106
    frosted 106
    gold or silver 106
Blue Jazz Cake 82
Blue Teddy Bear Cake 55
bootees, pressure piped 105
Border Piping 46–55:
    alternating shells 48
    bulbs 51
    dots, beads and pearls 52
    fleur-de-lis 48
    overpiping 52
    petal and leaf tube (tip) 54
    raised trellis 50
    rosettes 49
    scrolls 49
    shells 48
    stars 48
    starting 47
    twisted rope 49
broderie anglaise 67
brush embroidery 70
butterflies, stencilled 112

Cake Preparation 22–29:
    covering with marzipan 25
    improving 23
    levelling 24
    storing 23
cake board decoration 138
cake boards, designer 136
Cake Design 56–65:
    base colour 59
    colour schemes 59
    feature decoration 61
    overall balance 61
    plan 58
    shape 56
    size 57
cake pillars, designer 136
    coloured 137
    floral 137
    marbled 137
    textured 137

cake side effects 45, 65, 114:
    smocking 73
    stippled icing border 73
    sugar textured border 73
    two-colour comb scraper 73
cake supports 136
chick, pressure piped 103
clown:
    piped 107
    stencilled 115
Coating Techniques 30–39:
    adding colour to icing 30
    cake board 39
        cleaning 32
    consistency of icing 30
    drying between coats 33
    quick 38
    second and subsequent 34
    shaped cakes 35
        heart and petal 36
        horseshoe 36
        oblong 35
        octagonal and hexagonal 35
        oval 36
        triangular 35
    side, round cakes 31
    side, square cakes 32
    tidying top edge 32
    top, round and square cakes 33
collars:
    base 95
    cut-out sections 97
    filigree 98
    line and dot 98
    overlays 97
    picot dot edge 97
    scroll work 97
    types of 96
    under 97
colour:
    matching 135
    mixing 17, 135
    scheme 59
    spectrum 59
colourings 16
    colour pens 17
    liquid colours 16
    paste colours 16
    powder colours 17
compressors 118
consistency
    see royal icing
copyright infringement 63
cut scrapers
    see scrapers

daisy 77, 101
designs, transferring 64
dog 103, 109

embroidery:
    basic 66
    brush 70
    tube (tip) 67
enlargement and reduction of designs 63
Equipment 8–11
Exhibition Work 140–147:
    after the judging 147
    assembling typical cake 146
    cake and board coating 142, 143
    cake side coating 142
    cake top coating 143
    designing cake or plaque 141
    first steps 141
    judges, how they mark 147
    packing and exhibiting 146
    piping on cake side 144
    take-off marks 143
    technique tips 144

Filigree and Flowers 21st Cake 90
flower nails 75, 80
Flower Piping 74–81:
    Bess rose 77
    Christmas rose 78
    daffodil 77
    daisy 77, 101
    narcissus 77
    pansy 78
    primrose 78
    rose 79
    sweet pea 78
    using a flower nail 75
    without a flower nail 74
Frill and Tulle Flower Cake 12
frilling tubes (tips) 54

hearts, pressure piped 101
hearts, bells and flowers,
    stencilled 113

icing
    see royal icing
icing (confectioner's) sugar 13
improvers, icing 16

Jack-in-the-Box 132
judges, how they mark 147

leaves, piping 54, 80
Lemon Filigree Wedding Cake 40

Lettering 82–89:
  colour 84
  directly piped 86
  illuminated 87
  monograms 88
  position and spacing 85
  prefabricated plaques 87
  runout 87
  size 84
  stencilled 87
  style 83
  templates 158
line and dot 98
lines:
  avoiding breaking 42
  avoiding bulbs at ends 42
  avoiding curly 41
  holding piping bag 41
  piping adjacent 43
  piping curved 42
Linework 40–45:
  on side of cake 45
  starting 41
love birds 102
love birds and daisy chain 102
lover's knot 101

marzipan:
  calculating amount 26
  covering cake 25
    large cakes 29
    round cakes 26
    shaped cakes 29
    square cakes 29
masking materials (airbrushing) 119
Modelling 128–133
monograms 88
motor car with teddy 133

numerals 88
  templates 158

off-pieces, stencilled 111
Orange Rose Wedding Cake 22
outlining and flooding-in 92

overpiping:
  borders 52
  linework 43

packing and exhibiting 146
Painting 122–127:
  applying colour 124
  highlights 125
  outlines 125
  preparation 123
  shading 124
  starting 123
  textures 125
petal gazebo 130
Petal Gazebo Bride Cake 128
Pink Heart with Flowers 46
Pink Marble and Rose Cake 135
Pink Rabbit Cake 140
pin-pricking designs 64
piping bag, making 20
plaques:
  painted 127
  prefabricated 87
  runout 99
portions of cake, calculating 57
Pressure Piping 100–107

rabbit, pressure piped 103
rabbit runout figure 99
reduction and enlargement of
  designs 63
Retirement Cottage Cake 116
ribbon, attaching to board 138
robin, pressure piped 105
Royal Icing, About 12–21:
  adding colour 30
  competition quality 142
  consistency 15, 75
    adjusting for coating 30
  mixing coloured 19
  recipes 15
  storing 15
Rugby Club Cake 62
run-icing, making 91
  marbled effect 99
runouts and full collars, large 94

runouts, drying 94
Runout Work 90–99

santa, pressure piped 105
scrapers 10, 36–7, 73
scratched lines 44
Snow Cake with Skier 122
snowman, pressure piped 105
Stencilling 108–115:
  cleaning and maintenance 111
  cutting 110
  making 109
  using 110
stencilling on cake sides 114
stencils:
  multi-coloured 114
  textured 114
Stork and Bow Christening Cake 108
swan, pressure piped 103

take-off marks 34, 143
technique tips 144
teddy bear, pressure piped 104
Templates 148–158:
  for cake side, making 65
tracing designs 64
tube (tip) embroidery 67
  back stitch 68
  buttonhole, wheel 68
  chain stitch 68
  feather stitch 68
  fishbone stitch 68
  French knots 69
  herringbone 68
  lazy daisy 68
  long and short stitch 69
  plaques 69
  running stitch 68
  seed stitch 68
  stem stitch 68
tulle flower 129
21st ornament 129

wedge, cutting a 139
White Satin Bride Cake 100
Windmill Scene 121

FOR FURTHER INFORMATION

Merehurst is the leading publisher of cake decorating books and has an excellent range of titles to suit all levels. Please send for our free catalogue, stating the title of this book:-

UNITED KINGDOM
Marketing Department
Merehurst Ltd.
Ferry House
51–57 Lacy Road
London SW15 1PR
Tel: 081 780 1177
Fax: 081 780 1714

UNITED STATES OF AMERICA
Sterling Publishing Co. Inc.
387 Park Avenue South
New York NY 10016-8810
USA
Tel: (1) 212 532 7160
Fax: (1) 212 213 2495

AUSTRALIA
J. B. Fairfax Press Pty. Ltd.
80 McLachlan Avenue
Rushcutters Bay
NSW 2011
Tel: (61) 2 361 6366
Fax: (61) 2 360 6262

OTHER TERRITORIES
For further information contact:
Merehurst International Sales Department at United Kingdom address.